Programming with QuickBASIC

Wayne M. Zage

Ball State University


```
FOR I = 2 TO 3
PRINT "ENTER NEW"; CATEGORY$(I)
INPUT PAY
INCOME = INCOME + PAY
AMOUNT(I) = AMOUNT(I) + PAY
AMOUNT(4) = AMOUNT(4) + PAY
NEXT I
RETURN
EXPENSES:
PRINT "UPDATE EXPENSES"
PRINT
TOTALEXPENSE = 0
FOR I = 5 TO 16
PRINT "ENTER EXPENSE FOR"; CATEGORY$(I)
INPUT EXPENSE
AMOUNT(I) = AMOUNT(I) + EXPENSE
AMOUNT(17) = AMOUNT(17) + EXPENSE
TOTALEXPENSE = TOTALEXPENSE + EXPENSE
NEXT I
PRINT
RETURN
FINALREPORT:
BALANCE = INCOME - TOTALEXPENSE
PRINT USING A$; "THIS MONTH'S BALANCE", BALANCE
PRINT
PRINT "THE CUMULATIVE TOTALS:"
FOR I = 2 TO 4
PRINT USING A$; CATEGORY$(I), AMOUNT(I)
NEXT I
PRINT
FOR I = 5 TO 17
PRINT USING A$; CATEGORY$(I), AMOUNT(I)
NEXT I
...OUNT(1) = AMOUNT(1) + BALANCE
...SING A$; "NET CASH"; AMOUNT(1)
...OR OUTPUT AS #1
```

Mitchell McGRAW-HILL

New York St. Louis San Francisco Auckland Bogotá Caracas Lisbon London Madrid Mexico Milan Montreal New Delhi Paris San Juan Singapore Sydney Tokyo Toronto Watsonville

Mitchell **McGraw-Hill**
55 Penny Lane
Watsonville, CA 95076

Programming with QuickBASIC

4 5 6 7 8 9 0 MAL MAL 9 0 9 8 7 6 5 4

ISBN 0-07-073001-6

The sponsoring editor was Erika Berg.
The production was managed by Mitchell Publishing, Inc.
The production was supervised by Betty Drury.
The cover designer was John Edeen.
The printer and binder was Malloy Lithographing, Inc.

Library of Congress Catalog Card Number 90-64377
This book is printed on acid-free paper.

CONTENTS

CHAPTER FOUR. ARRAYS

CHAPTER FIVE. CHARACTER STRING FUNCTIONS

CHAPTER SIX. FORMATTING OPTIONS

CHAPTER SEVEN. DATA FILES

PREFACE

Programming With QuickBASIC is designed for a course that has program development as one of its major components. The text can also be used as a self-teaching tool for any person who has access to a computer that has QuickBASIC. This book gives the reader a complete and efficient view of QuickBASIC and, in general, is suitable for anyone who wants an introduction to programming concepts and the QuickBASIC programming language.

Objectives

The objectives of this text are to:

- Provide the reader with a sufficient overview of the QuickBASIC programming language to enable the reader to write programs and to solve problems using QuickBASIC in a variety of application areas.
- Provide enough specific examples of QuickBASIC statements, program segments, and complete programs to allow a new programmer to feel comfortable with QuickBASIC. Notes are provided after each of the major programs to help the reader understand the intricacies of the programming statements.
- Aid the reader in analyzing programming problems. This is accomplished through the discussion of the logic of the solution for each of the major programs in the text.
- Teach sound programming techniques through examples and through detailed discussion of their value in program development.

Distinguishing Features of the Text

The text materials have been developed and classroom tested over an eight-year period at Ball State University and Purdue University. No previous familiarity with computers is assumed. The text begins with a presentation of terms used in programming and with fundamental statements in the QuickBASIC programming language. Complete QuickBASIC programs start appearing early in the text and are developed through a step-by-step approach in which the reader is carefully taken through the logical development of each program. This step-by-step development of programs is retained throughout the text to enable the reader to focus on the creative process of analyzing problems and designing programs.

Good programming practices are stressed throughout the text. Emphasis is placed on structured programming and the QuickBASIC constructs that enhance program modularization and incremental development. Topics such as the use of mnemonic variable names, the initialization of variables, the selection of appropriate test data, and the rationale behind making backups of data files before modification are discussed.

The programs in the text range in difficulty from short examples to "see what the code does," to more sophisticated examples that even the experienced programmer should find interesting and challenging. Some programs in the text are revisited after new QuickBASIC statements are presented to enhance the earlier version. The program themes are taken from a wide variety of fields, including business, probability and simulations, education, computer-assisted instruction, and personal applications. Common applications familiar to most readers, such as compound interest, payroll, a checking account, employee lists, personal expense records, car rentals, coin tossing, dice games, sorting class test scores, playing tic-tac-toe, and ordering fast food, are used in an effort to apply QuickBASIC to interesting problems, not simply teach QuickBASIC syntax.

Review exercises, lab exercises, and programming problems are included in each chapter. The review exercises are designed to enable the reader to review the terms and the QuickBASIC programming statements presented, as well as check the reader's understanding of the programs in the text. The lab exercises are designed to get the student actively involved in working through the concepts in the text. They are meant to be completed by the student, one-on-one with a computer, with little or no instructor intervention. Space is provided in the text so that the student can record the answers to the questions for later review. These sections can be assigned as extra homework problems or can be used by an instructor who wants to provide a weekly hands-on lab session as part of the structure of a course. The programming problems ask the student either to enhance a program given in the text or to design and code a completely new program that uses the QuickBASIC statements presented in the current and previous chapters. These problems are written not only to instruct but also to entertain by providing a theme or story in which to develop a program.

Acknowledgments

I would like to express my sincere thanks to all of the people who helped develop this text. I would like to thank Professor Dolores M. Zage and Dr. H. E. Dunsmore at Purdue University for their comprehensive and insightful reviews and comments throughout the development of the manuscript. In particular, Dr. Dunsmore's meticulous effort is reflected on many of the pages in this text. I would like to thank Marcia Franck at Ball State University for testing the programs found in this text on an IBM PS/2 computer. Special thanks go to Georgia Conarroe for editing the manuscript and for writing the PIC commands on the UNIX system to generate the flowcharts and pictures seen in the text. I would also like to thank Kay Nelson for her copy editing work. At Mitchell/McGraw-Hill, I would like to thank the Informations Systems editor Erika C. Berg for initiating this project and for her editorial assistance and continuous encouragement during the writing of this text.

CHAPTER ONE

THE FUNDAMENTALS OF QUICK-BASIC

"Indeed, what is there that does not appear marvelous when it comes to our knowledge for the first time. How many things, too, are looked upon as quite impossible until they have been actually effected?" (Pliny the Elder, A.D. 23–79, *Natural History*, Book VII, Section 6.)

A. INTRODUCTION

We often think of a computer as a machine that can process data at a rate many times that of a human being. It is really a combination of hardware and software that allows a computer to function. *Hardware* is the "nuts and bolts" of computers, including monitors, keyboards, disk drives, memory boards, and integrated circuitry. In short, it is the machinery that enables input, processing, and output to occur.

Software consists of sets of instructions, or programs, that direct the hardware in the execution of tasks. Special programming languages, that are very "English-like" in their appearance, have been developed to permit programmers to write instructions that are easy for humans to understand. Examples of these languages are COBOL, Fortran, C, Pascal, and QuickBASIC.

Our goal in this text is to focus on QuickBASIC, which is a modern version of one of the most widely used programming languages and one that is relatively easy to learn, namely the BASIC (Beginner's All-purpose Symbolic Instruction Code) programming language. QuickBASIC will be used to write software programs in a wide variety of business, educational, and personal applications. This chapter begins with a presentation of some of the terms and concepts related to computers and to programming languages. We'll also discuss the essentials of the QuickBASIC programming environment. Then, after some specific QuickBASIC programming statements are presented, the reader is guided through several QuickBASIC programs.

B. MAJOR COMPONENTS OF A COMPUTER SYSTEM

As we discuss the QuickBASIC programming language (which we will at times abbreviate as QB), it is sometimes necessary to refer to various parts of a computer system, such as primary memory, secondary memory, and input/output devices. In this section, these and the other major components of a computer system are introduced.

A computer system can be depicted as shown in Figure 1.1. The *input device* allows communication from the user to the computer. Through this component of the system, a programmer can enter programming statements or data into the computer. A common input device found in all microcomputer systems is the keyboard.

Output devices allow communication from the computer to the user. This communication may be a line-by-line display of a computer program, the results of executing a program, or graphics such as curves, bar graphs, and pie charts. Video display terminals, printers, and plotters are examples of output devices.

The heart of the computer system is the *central processing unit (CPU)*. Inside the CPU, we find three major components, namely primary memory, the arithmetic and logic unit, and the control unit. *Primary memory*, also known as main memory, provides the CPU with temporary storage for programs and data. This is a volatile storage location in that when the machine is turned off, the information is gone. A computer program resides in primary memory when it is being executed. In the case of microcomputers, the size of primary memory is given in a unit called bytes and is typically in the range from 64K bytes to 512K bytes (K = 1024).

The *arithmetic and logic* unit performs all of the arithmetic operations (addition, subtraction, multiplication, and division) and the logic operations (greater than, less than, equal to) needed in a computer program. A logic operation is a comparison between two pieces of data. Depending on the outcome of such comparisons, the computer can take alternative actions within a program.

The control unit acts essentially as a ''traffic police officer'' in the computer because its major tasks are to direct the operation of the CPU components and to control the flow of programs and data in and out of primary memory. The control unit performs these tasks by reading and interpreting program instructions.

Secondary memory, also called secondary storage, is the component of a computer system where programs can be stored in a permanent fashion. This is non-volatile memory; information stored here is not lost when the machine is turned off. From secondary storage, a program can be retrieved, loaded into primary memory, and executed or modified. Secondary storage space is needed simply because primary memory in a computer is limited and only of a temporary nature. Secondary storage media include magnetic tapes, hard disks, and floppy disks. Secondary memory in these forms has virtually unlimited capacity and is relatively inexpensive.

C. USING THE QUICKBASIC ENVIRONMENT

You will soon be entering, editing, running, and saving QB programs in a sophisticated environment designed to make your programming as easy as possible. The QB environment contains, among other entities, menus, windows, dialog boxes, and a full-screen editor. In this section, we discuss the essential features of the QB environment, which as you'll see, is very easy to use. For a complete discussion of the environment, consult your QB reference manual.

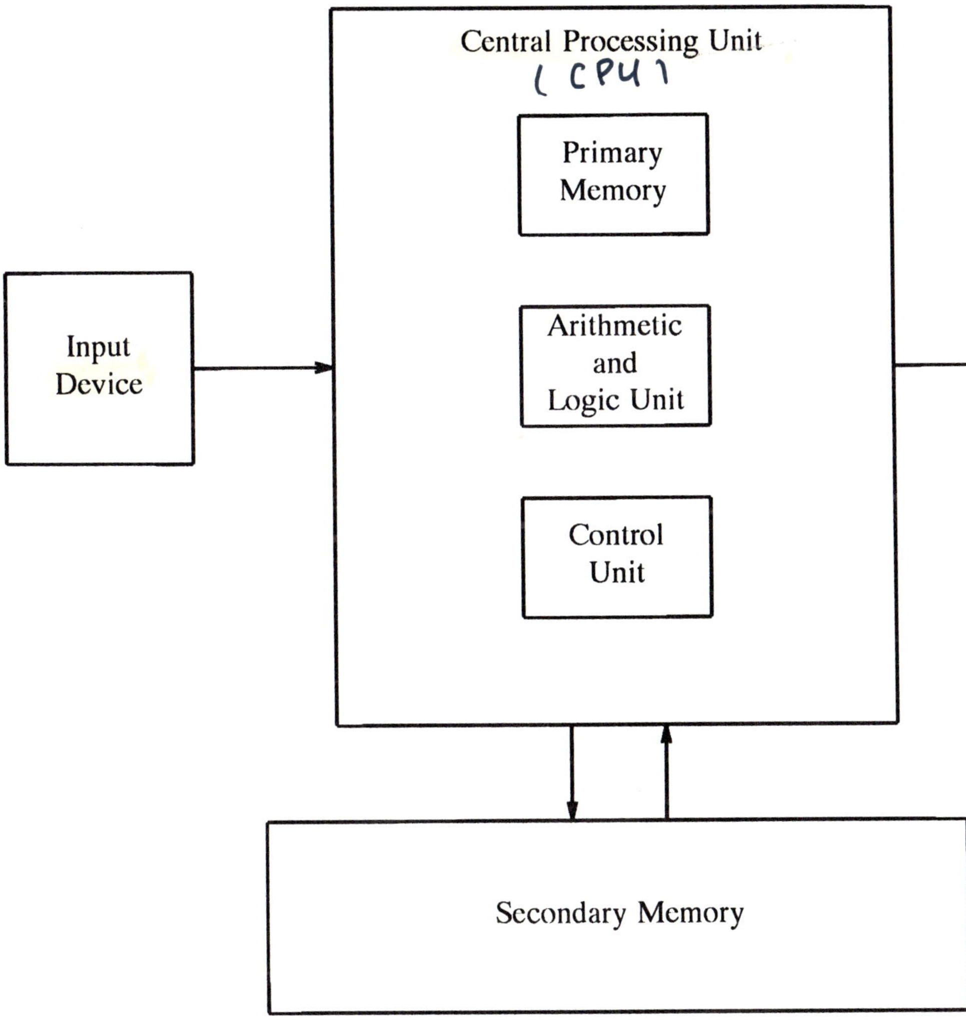

Figure 1.1. Major Components of a Computer System

Using the Editor to Enter a Program

When you start up QB, you'll use an initial screen as shown in Figure 1.2. At this point you could immediately start typing in a program, which would be visible in the relatively large area called the *view window*. You'll note that the screen contains a *title bar* that displays the name of a program in main memory. (It currently says "Untitled".) The top row of the screen contains the names of menus that are used for such functions as running a program, saving a program, and starting a new program. The *immediate window* is used to test single statements of QB and see the results "immediately".

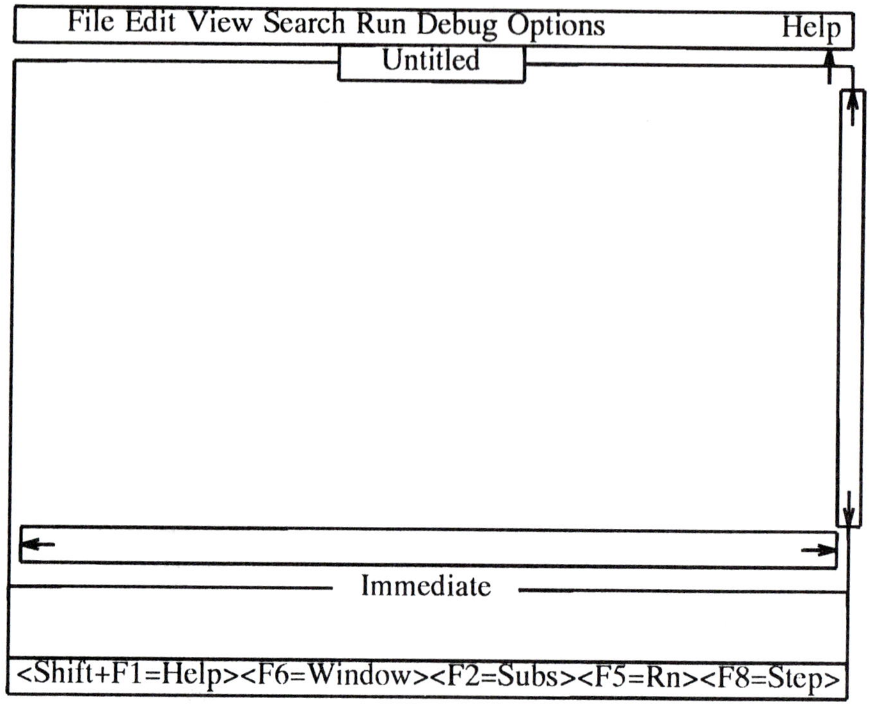

Figure 1.2. The Initial QuickBASIC Screen

Although we haven't discussed any QB statements formally yet, you can type in a single PRINT statement and then use this short example of a QB program to illustrate some of the features of the QB environment. (The PRINT statement will be discussed in detail later in this chapter.) So, type in the one-line QB program shown below, putting your name in place of "BOB".

```
PRINT "MY NAME IS BOB"
```

Running a Program

As you probably guessed, if you ran this program (yes, this is a complete QB program) you would expect to see the statement "MY NAME IS BOB" appear on the screen. To run the program, you need to "pull down" the Run menu. All menus are accessed in QB by pressing the Alt key and then the first letter of the menu name. So press Alt-R, and you find that your screen looks like Figure 1.3.

You'll note that the top selection on the menu is highlighted. You can move the highlight to other options on the menu by using the arrow keys. To run your program, you need only highlight "Start" and then select that option by pressing the Enter key. The program will execute, with the results displayed not in the view window, but rather on an output screen, similar to what you see in Figure 1.4. Pressing any key returns control to the QB edit screen.

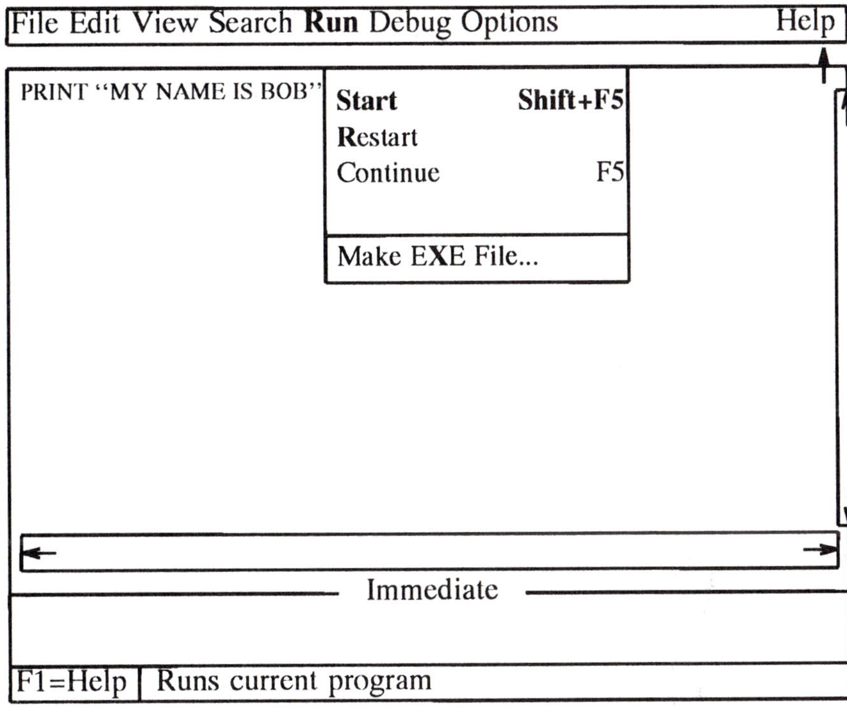

Figure 1.3. The Run Menu

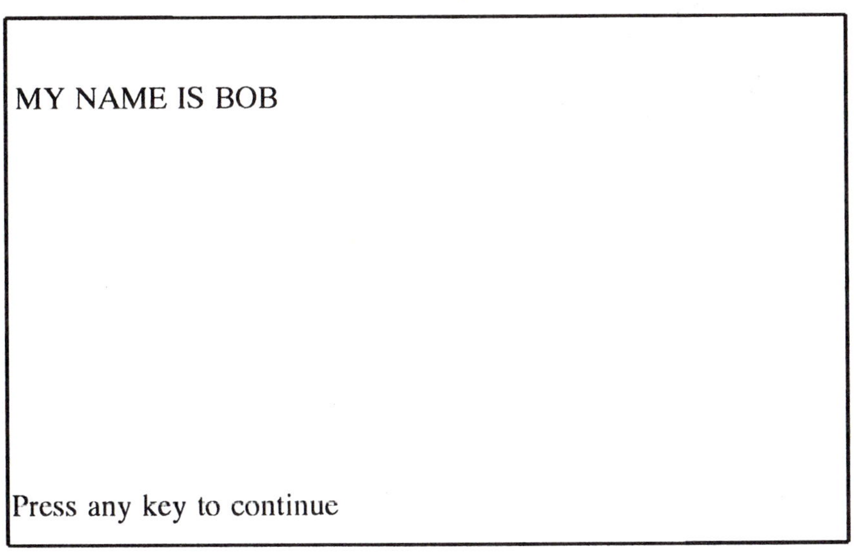

Figure 1.4. Results of the Program on an Output Screen

Editing a Program

QB comes with a full-screen editor that allows you to easily navigate (move the cursor) through a program. You can move the cursor by using the arrow keys and the Home and End keys, as well as the PgDn and PgUp keys. Edit this one-line program by adding Bob's (or your) last name. In our example, we'll add the last name Anderson. To insert text in the middle of a line, move the cursor to the desired position, type in the text, and then move the cursor to the end of the line by pressing the End key. And so, with the cursor under the closing quotation marks, simply type a space followed by Anderson (or your last name) and press the End key. You can now add a second line stating Bob's city of residence. Press Enter to move the cursor to the next line. (If you did not press the End key as suggested above, pressing Enter split the line into two pieces. To make the repair, press the Backspace key and then the End key.) Then type in the statement (enter your own hometown if you wish)

```
PRINT  "HOMETOWN, USA"
```

You can now run your two-line program by pulling down the Run menu (pressing Alt-R) and selecting the Start option. You should see two more lines printed on the output screen.

If you need to delete a character from inside a line, move the cursor under that character and press the Del key. You can also move the cursor just to the right of the character you want to delete and press the Backspace key. If you need to delete an entire line, place the cursor anywhere on that line and press Ctrl-Y.

Saving a Program

To show you how to save a program (i.e., store it on a disk), let's save the two-line program under the name FIRSTTRY. To save your program,

1. Pull down the File menu (press Alt-F).
2. Press the down arrow key until you highlight "Save As...".
3. Select this option by pressing Enter. At this point a dialog box opens, as shown in Figure 1.5. QB simply needs more information before it can save the program, and so it is asking for a file name.
4. Type the name FIRSTTRY and press Enter.

The dialog box will disappear and you'll see your two-line program with the title FIRSTTRY.BAS in the title bar area. (QB adds the extension BAS automatically.)

Starting a New Program

To begin a new program, you would need to clear out main memory and either load a file (from secondary storage) that already exists or start typing in new QB statements. To erase FIRSTTRY.BAS,

1. Select the File menu (press Alt-F). The highlight will already be on "New Program".
2. Press Enter.

The program is erased from main memory, the edit screen clears, and the title bar again displays the word "Untitled". You could now type in a new program or bring into main memory a previous program from storage, even FIRSTTRY! Recall that since the program was previously saved in secondary memory, the program remained stored there even though you erased it from main memory. If you wanted to load FIRSTTRY, you'd simply select the Load File option from the File menu. You'll see a dialog box appear in which you can type FIRSTTRY and press Enter. The file will then again be available for execution or modification.

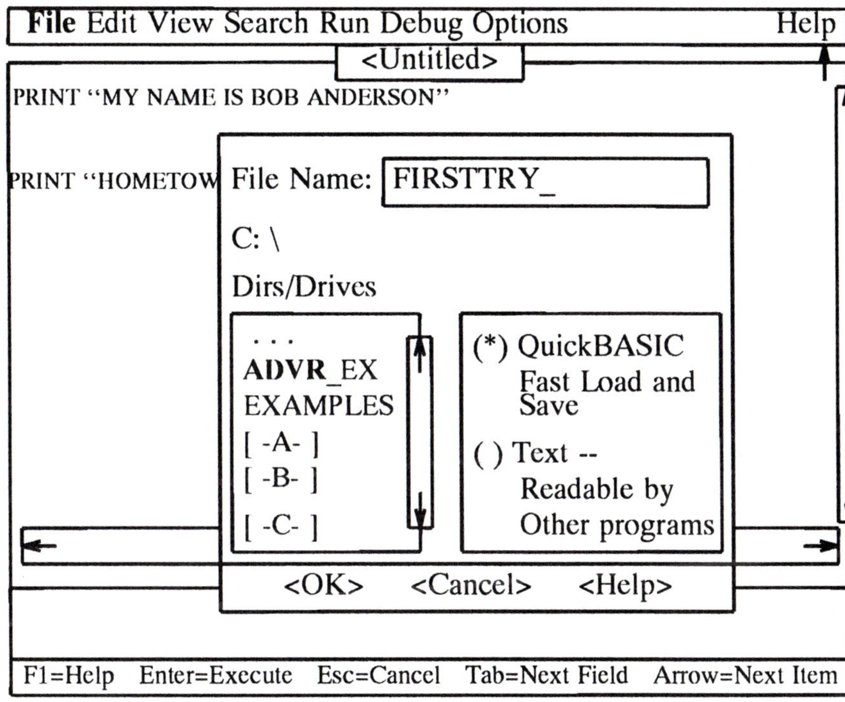

Figure 1.5. The File Name Dialog Box

Exiting QuickBASIC

To exit QuickBASIC, pull down the File menu and select Exit. If there is a file in primary memory that has not been saved, QuickBASIC will ask if you want to save it. You can move between your choices by pressing the Tab key, and you can select your choice by again pressing Enter. After you press Enter, you will have exited QuickBASIC and the DOS prompt will appear.

And so you have seen how to create, edit, run, and save a program in the QB environment. You have also seen how you can reload into main memory a program previously stored and how to exit QB. You'll be performing all of these functions often, and as you do, the QB environment with its menus, windows, and dialog boxes will soon be very familiar to you.

D. QUICKBASIC LANGUAGE COMPONENTS

In this section some of the terminology that is used frequently by people programming in QuickBASIC (and by computer programmers in general) is defined. A knowledge of these terms is essential for you to thoroughly understand this text.

Constants

Constants are values that do not change during the execution of a program. The two major categories of constants are numbers and character strings. Consider the following examples:

	Constant	Type
1.	73	Numeric (integer)
2.	-14.6	Numeric (decimal)
3.	''LESSON ONE''	Character
4.	''1991''	Character
5.	4.659E+4	Numeric (exponential)
6.	7.612E-3	Numeric (exponential)

The numeric constants can be written as decimals or integers, and when very large or very small numbers are involved, an exponential notation can be used. (See examples 5 and 6 above.) The E represents base 10 and the signed number following the E is the power to which 10 is raised. Note that

$$4.659E+4 = 4.659 \times 10^{4} = 46590$$

and

$$7.612E-3 = 7.612 \times 10^{-3} = .007612$$

A *character string constant* is any sequence of letters of the alphabet, numbers, and special characters enclosed in quotation marks. Note the difference between the integer constant 1991, which may be used in arithmetic operations, and the character string constant ''1991'', which may represent a calendar year and would never be part of an arithmetic operation. Thus ''1991'' would never be added to or subtracted from a numeric value; it is simply a string of characters, much like the string ''ABCD''.

Variables

Variables are commonly used in almost all walks of life. In elementary school a child may be taught that the relationship between the number of feet f and the equivalent number of inches i can be expressed as

$$i = 12 * f$$

In this case, every time the number of feet increases by 1, the number of inches increases by 12. Since the number of feet f and the resulting number of inches i can vary, f and i are called variables.

As another example, consider the following relationship that can be used to compute the weekly pay for a person employed at an hourly rate:

$$\text{PAY} = \text{RATE} * \text{HOURS}$$

As the value of either RATE or HOURS varies, so does the weekly pay represented by the variable PAY.

A person may have a savings plan where money is earning interest compounded annually. In this situation, starting with a principal of P dollars earning i percent interest per year, the resulting amount A after n years is given by the equation

$$A = P * (1 + i)^n$$

A different value of the variable *P*, *i*, or *n* results in a different total amount of dollars represented by the variable *A*.

In computer programming, too, variables represent quantities in a program. A variable may vary from one point to another in a program, or in fact, once given a value, it may remain fixed for the entire execution of a program. More specifically, the term *variable* refers to any name used in a program to represent a specific location in the computer's primary memory. In other words, a variable represents a place where data can be stored. Values are assigned to variables by using particular QB statements in a computer program. (See the discussion of the LET and INPUT statements in the next section, the presentation of the READ/DATA statements in Chapter Two and the discussion of data files in Chapter Seven.)

Programming languages generally have rules that must be followed when naming variables. One rule that is common to many versions of BASIC and is followed in this text is that variable names can be up to 40 significant characters in length. (You can consult a reference manual to determine if variable names are governed by this rule or a more restricted one for your particular system.) Another rule in naming variables is that the first character must be a letter of the alphabet. You should select mnemonic variable names when writing programs. Note the difference between the character string constant "COST" and the numeric variable COST.

Just as there are two types of constants, there are also two types of variables: numeric and character string. The term *string* is a shortened version of the term *character string*. Character string variable names must end in a dollar sign ($) in QB.

There is a list of words in QB, called ***reserved words***, that have a special meaning to the QB compiler, and thus cannot be used as variable names. Refer to a QB reference manual for a list of the reserved words in QuickBASIC.

Data Types

There may be times when you'll want to choose the types of your data carefully in order to gain a certain level of precision in your program. Figure 1.6 illustrates in more detail the types of constants and variables available in the QB programming language.

In the numeric category, you see integer (a number with no fractional part), which includes values in the range -32,768 to 32,767, and long integer, which extends the range of values from -2,147,483,648 to 2,147,483,647. The floating-point constants may have fractional parts or may be integers simply too large to be handled as a whole number. The range of floating-point single-precision numbers is -3.4E+38 to 3.4E+38. For floating-point double precision, the range is -1.8D+308 to 1.8D+308. (The exponential indicator for double precision is D rather than E.) Double-precision numbers are accurate to 15 digits.

Most string variables can hold variable-length strings, which means that the length of the string stored in that variable can change. With a fixed-length string variable, you store only character data of a fixed length, which must be declared in a QB program.

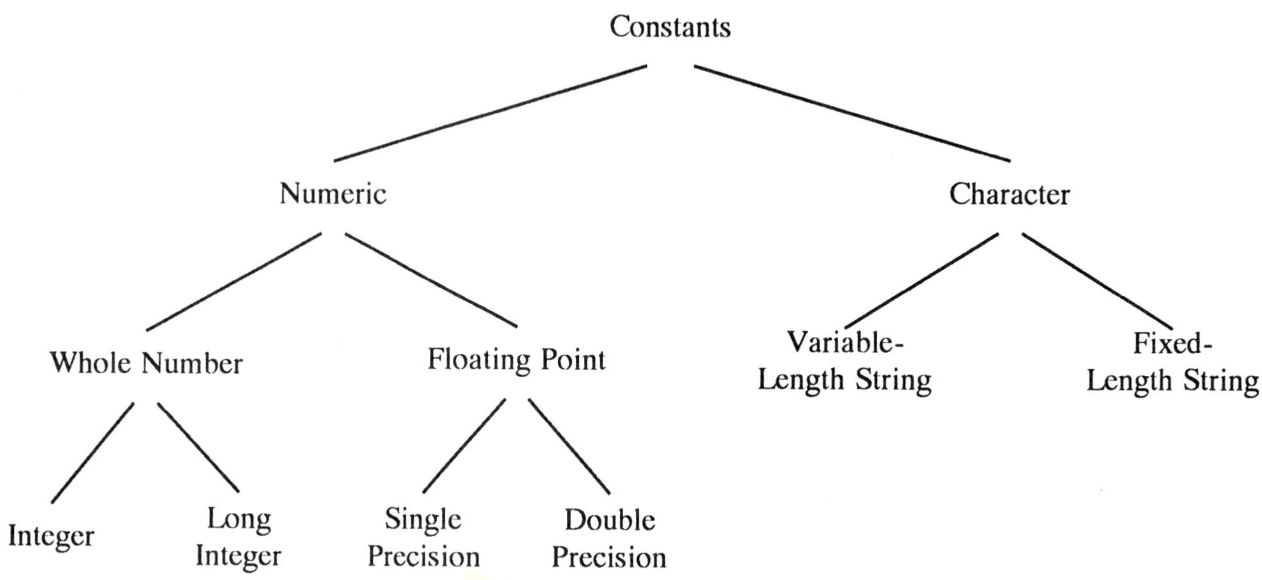

Figure 1.6. Data Types in QuickBASIC

In QuickBASIC, there are several different ways to give your data a distinct data type. One of these is to use type-declaration suffix characters, as shown in Table 1.1. By appending one of the suffixes %, &, !, #, $ to a variable name, you describe the data type for that variable. You'll note that the dollar sign, as mentioned earlier, must be the suffix in a character string variable name. (It is repeated here to provide a complete list of suffixes available in QB in Table 1.1.)

Suffix	Variable Type	Example
%	Integer	OrderNumber%
&	Long Integer	DistanceInSpace&
!	Single Precision	CheckBalance!
#	Double Precision	NationDebt#
$	Variable Length String	YourName$

Table 1.1

In general, you choose the simplest data type to get the processing job done. If you are working with integers, you will most often simply use the integer data type constants and variables. If you are working with decimal values, single precision will generally suffice. And for your character string data, the variable-length string type is normally adequate. Using more precision than necessary will use more computer memory and slow down the processing speed with no gain in the calculation accuracy required. If no type is explicitly stated, the default for whole numbers is integer; for floating-point numbers, single precision; and for character data, variable string length.

Relational Operators

A number of *relational operators* are needed in QB to form what are called *logical expressions*. Table 1.2 lists the relational operators and their meanings, as well as the equivalent mathematical symbols.

Relational Operator	Meaning	Mathematical Equivalent
>	greater than	$>$
<	less than	$<$
>=	greater than or equal to	$\geq$
<=	less than or equal to	$\leq$
=	equal to	$=$
< >	not equal to	$\neq$

Table 1.2

Arithmetic Operators

Arithmetic operators are the symbols used to denote the usual arithmetic operations of addition, subtraction, multiplication, division, and exponentiation. Table 1.3 compares the arithmetic symbol for each of these operations with the corresponding symbol used in QB.

Arithmetic Operation	Usual Arithmetic Symbol	Symbol Used in QB	Example	Result
Addition	+	+	4 + 7	11
Subtraction	-	-	16.5 - 4	12.5
Multiplication	· or x	*	3.5*4.5	15.75
Division	÷	/	9.3/3.1	3
Exponentiation	A^B	^	2 ^ 3	8

Table 1.3

You can mix data types in arithmetic expressions. The result is expressed in the simplest data type possible. (For an example, see the division problem in Table 1.3.)

Expressions

Expressions can be arithmetic or logical. An *arithmetic expression is* an arithmetic formula, consisting of a sequence of variables, constants, and arithmetic operators that is to be evaluated. Examples are

```
X + 3
A + B - 5
C * D / 2
.5 * B * H
```

Note that when all of the variables in an arithmetic expression are replaced by their current values, the expression evaluates to a single number.

A *logical expression* is a sequence of variables, constants, relational operators, and connectives that always has a value of either true or false. Examples include

A > B
X + Y <= 0
A < B AND B > C

Note that when an expression such as A > B is encountered in a program, the current values of A and B determine whether the expression is true or false.

Arithmetic and logical expressions appear frequently in programming statements. For example, the last arithmetic expression listed above can be used to calculate the area A of a triangle given the base B and the height H, using the equation

A = .5 * B * H

Logical expressions, such as A > B, have a value of either true or false and can be used to establish the condition under which a task is performed in a program. For example, using the logical expression A > B, you can cause a branch to a specific set of statements in a program whenever this expression is true (i.e., whenever the value of A is greater than the value of B).

You may realize that we use logical expressions daily. For example, a young man might say "If I finish my homework before 7:00 P.M., then I'll play volleyball tonight". Then, if he finishes his homework before 7:00 P.M. (i.e., the logical expression "homework finished before 7:00 P.M." is true), he can proceed to the volleyball courts.

Statements

A *statement* is the fundamental unit in a computer program. Each QB statement includes a QB keyword that specifies the action you want to perform, and usually additional information such as parameters or expressions. Line numbers are optional in QB. The order of execution of statements is determined by the listing order in a program. The following QB statement instructs the computer to print the value of the variable A:

```
PRINT A
```

We shall see that alphanumeric labels are very useful in identifying a statement or the beginning of a set of statements in a QB program. In fact, labels are superior to line numbers because an alphanumeric label can convey meaningful information about the program. For example, consider the following labels and the information they convey:

```
PrintRoutine:
ErrorMessage:
FindingAnswer:
Signoff:
```

Note that a colon is used to terminate a label.

E. ORDER OF OPERATIONS

The computer must have a set of rules for determining how to evaluate an arithmetic expression containing more than one operator. For example, should the expression 3 + 5 * 2 be evaluated by doing the addition before the multiplication?

$$3 + 5 * 2 = 8 * 2 = 16$$

Or should the multiplication be completed before the addition?

$$3 + 5 * 2 = 3 + 10 = 13$$

To remove ambiguity in these situations, the following hierarchy of operations has been established:

(1) Operations within parentheses
(2) Exponentiation
(3) Multiplication or division
(4) Addition or subtraction

Operations within parentheses are always completed first. Then all exponentiations are performed, proceeding from left to right in an expression. After that, all multiplications and divisions (these are at the same level in the hierarchy) are evaluated in order from left to right, followed by all additions and subtractions from left to right. When a set of parentheses is used within another set of parentheses, the innermost expression is evaluated first. Thus the answer to the problem posed above is 13. Consider also the following examples:

1. *Evaluate* 3 + 7 * 2 + 3.

This problem involves only the operations of multiplication and addition. Multiplication has a higher priority than addition, and therefore 7 * 2 is evaluated first. Then the additions are performed in order from left to right. We obtain

$$3 + \underbrace{7 * 2} + 3$$

$$\underbrace{3 + 14} + 3$$

$$\underbrace{17 + 3}$$

$$20$$

2. *Evaluate* (3 + 7) * 2 + 3.

The operation within parentheses is done first, then the multiplication, and then finally 3 is added.

(3 + 7) * 2 + 3

10 * 2 + 3

20 + 3

23

3. *Evaluate* (3 + 7) * (2 + 3).

The operations in parentheses are evaluated first, in order from left to right. The multiplication is performed last.

(3 + 7) * 2 + 3

10 * (2 + 3)

10 * 5

50

Compare examples 1, 2 and 3 to see the effects of the use of parentheses.

4. *Evaluate* 2 + 3 * 6 / 9 - 5 * 5.

The five operations in the above expression are all from the two lowest levels in the hierarchy of operations. The two multiplications and the division operation will be evaluated first, in order from left to right. Afterwards, the addition and subtraction will take place.

2 + 3 * 6 / 9 – 5 * 5

2 + 18 / 9 – 5 * 5

2 + 2 – 5 * 5

2 + 2 – 25

4 – 25

– 21

5. *Evaluate* 3 * 2 ^ 3 * (4 + 1) + 1 / 4.

Operations from all four levels of the hierarchy are included in this example. You are encouraged to follow carefully the detailed steps below.

```
3 * 2 ^ 3 * (4 + 1) + 1 / 4

3 * 2 ^ 3 * 5 + 1 / 4

3 * 8 * 5 + 1 / 4

24 * 5 + 1 / 4

120 + 1 / 4

120 + .25

120.25
```

F. STEPS IN WRITING A PROGRAM

In this text, QB programs are written to solve a variety of problems. As the problems and the programs become more sophisticated, you will find that it is important to design a computer program (whether it is written in QuickBASIC or in any other language, for that matter) in some systematic way. This programming process can be characterized as a sequence of five steps:

(1) Describe the problem.

(2) Design the general logic of the solution.

(3) Write the program in a computer language (which will be referred to as writing code for the program).

(4) Test and debug the program.

(5) Document the program.

Step 2 listed above may at times be the most difficult of the programming steps. A programmer develops the general logic of a solution by designing an *algorithm*, which is a step-by-step procedure, to solve a particular problem. For example, to obtain a close approximation of the number of gallons of paint needed to paint the ceiling of a large hall, the algorithm would consist of the following steps:

(1) Multiply the length (in feet) of the hall by the width (in feet) of the hall to obtain the square footage of the ceiling.

(2) Divide the number of square feet by 400 (assuming one gallon will cover 400 square feet) to obtain the number of gallons needed.

Although the solution to this problem consists of only two steps, it illustrates the importance of establishing the proper order of steps in an algorithm. Notice also that we are calculating the amount of paint for the ceiling by dealing with the square footage of the floor! The idea of using some things to stand for others to make your job easier is a typical technique used in programming.

We will follow the five-step process listed above in the programming examples in this text.

G. SOME ELEMENTARY QUICKBASIC STATEMENTS

Before programs can be designed using the five steps listed above, some of the statements in the QuickBASIC programming language must be introduced.

In this section, the seven elementary QB statements REM, CLS, LET, PRINT, LPRINT, INPUT, and END are presented.

The REM Statement

The remark, or REM, statement is a non-executable (provides no information to the computer) statement used by a programmer to provide information to someone reading the list of statements in the program. The remarks may explain the purpose of the program, the use of variables in the code, the assumptions made in the development of the program, the intricacies of difficult program segments, or they may simply be used to incorporate the programmer's name and the current date in the code. REM statements can be placed anywhere in a program.

The general format of the REM statement is:

```
REM comment
```

In QB, the apostrophe can be substituted for the REM keyword.

For example, at the beginning of a program designed to calculate weekly pay for an individual, we might find the following REM statements:

```
REM  COMPANY XYZ
REM  PAYROLL PROGRAM
REM  CREATED BY D. LENZ
REM  INPUT IS NUMBER OF HOURS WORKED AND RATE
REM  OUTPUT IS PAY FOR THE WEEK.
```

The REM statement is truly a comment line in your program. QB does not check a REM statement for misspelled words. If you put REM in front of a statement that you mean to be executed, it will not be executed.

The CLS Statement

Screen output from a program is easier to read if the screen has been cleared beforehand. The CLS (CLear Screen) statement clears the screen and moves the cursor to the upper-left corner. Its format is

```
CLS
```

The LET Statement

The LET statement, also called the assignment statement, assigns values to variables. Its general format is

LET variable = expression

where the expression can consist of a constant, another variable, string functions or an arithmetic formula to be evaluated. In QB, the word LET may be omitted. The expression on the right of the equal sign is always evaluated first and then the resulting value is assigned to the variable listed on the left of the equal sign. Thus, the flow of information is from right to left! Below are some examples of QB LET statements.

STATEMENT	*OUTCOME*
LET T = 7	The value 7 is assigned to the variable T.
LET TOTAL = R + 9	The sum of R plus 9 is assigned to the variable TOTAL.
PAY = RATE * HOURS	The product of the values of RATE and HOURS is assigned to the variable PAY.
LET X = B ^ 2	The value of B raised to the second power is assigned to the variable X.
A$ = "BOB"	The character string BOB is assigned to the character string variable A$.
LET N = N + 1	The current value of N is increased by 1 and then this new value is assigned to the variable N. In effect, this statement increments N by 1.

A note on the last example: Mathematically, the equation N = N + 1 has no solution. However, the QB statement

LET N = N + 1

is valid because the assignment of a value to N is done *after* the expression on the right is evaluated.

The PRINT Statement

The PRINT statement is designed to allow you to see a display of numerical data or character strings on the screen when a program is executed. Using the PRINT statement, you can print out the values of variables, character strings, or the results of arithmetic expressions. Its general form is as follows:

PRINT list of variables constants and/or expressions

For example, the statement

PRINT 7,9,3

would result in the output

```
7             9             3
```

whereas

```
PRINT 7;10;15
```

produces the output

```
 7  10  15
```

The comma and semicolon delimiters in the PRINT statement not only separate the data to be displayed but also help format the output on the printed page. A print line is divided into zones (also called fields) that vary in width from 14 to 18 character positions, depending on the BASIC interpreter being used. The first PRINT statement above would place one number in each of the first three zones. More precisely, assuming a width of 14 characters per zone and allowing a space in each zone for a minus sign for a negative number, the output would appear in the second, fifteenth, and twenty-ninth character positions. On the other hand, the use of semicolons places the numbers next to one another (again allowing spaces for minus signs) and thus the second PRINT statement gives a condensed output as shown above.

To print the numbers 7, 9, and 3 vertically (in the same column), you would use three PRINT statements:

```
PRINT 7
PRINT 9
PRINT 3
```

These statements would provide a vertical display because every PRINT statement makes QuickBASIC print on a new line. Therefore, the above statements provide output on three different lines with the numbers lining up in the same column.

For the payroll program, the programmer would want to prompt the user at the terminal that he or she is to enter a pay rate and the number of hours worked. This could be accomplished with the statement

```
PRINT "ENTER RATE AND HOURS WORKED."
```

which would result in the literal (character string) enclosed in quotes being displayed.

Literals and numerical values can, of course, be the output of a single PRINT statement. Furthermore, expressions can be evaluated within a PRINT statement. For example, if the value of A is 7 and the value of B is 12 when the statement

```
PRINT "THE SUM IS "; A + B
```

is encountered, the resulting output would be

THE SUM IS 19

As a final example, consider the statement

PRINT

As you might guess, the output is a blank line. The use of PRINT statements with no items listed is a common formatting technique to insert blank lines in the output of a program.

The LPRINT Statement

The LPRINT statement sends output from a program to a printer instead of to a screen. All of the rules that apply to the PRINT statement hold for the LPRINT statement as well. The general form of this statement is

LPRINT list of variables constants and/or expressions

The INPUT Statement

You have seen that the LET statement is one way to assign values to variables in a program. A second approach is to use the INPUT statement, which allows interaction between the computer program and the user of the program. Generally, the user at a terminal responds to a prompt asking for information required at that point in a program. The response is given while the program is executing. The general format of the INPUT statement is as follows:

INPUT variable list

The following are examples:

```
INPUT X
INPUT A, B
INPUT A$
```

If these three lines were consecutive lines in a program, then they could also be replaced with the single statement

INPUT X, A, B, A$

Note that the user would be required to insert three numerical values and one character string, in that order, in response to this statement. The data and the variable types (numeric or character) must agree.

For the program designed to calculate weekly pay based on a pay RATE and the number of HOURS worked, you could use

INPUT RATE, HOURS

Whenever you use the INPUT statement, be sure to precede it with a prompt in a PRINT statement telling the user what data need to be entered. For example, the preceding INPUT statement could follow the prompt

PRINT "ENTER RATE AND HOURS WORKED."

The END Statement

This statement not only indicates the *logical* end of the program to a person reading the lines of code, but it is also used to terminate program execution in the computer. It often appears as the last statement in a program. (We shall see that even though subprograms often appear physically after an END statement in the main program, the END statement will still designate the end of the logic flow in a program.) Its format is:

END

Some versions of BASIC, such as QuickBASIC, do not require the use of an END statement in a program.

H. FIRST EXAMPLE OF A PROGRAM

Up to now, a payroll program has been alluded to and lines that might be appropriate for this application have been suggested. The entire program following the five steps in the programming process listed earlier is now presented.

Program 1.

Step 1. Describe the problem.

Company XYZ wants to use its computer to calculate the pay for its hourly employees. The pay rate and the number of hours worked for each employee will be entered at a terminal. The output should consist of the rate, hours worked, and total pay for that individual.

Step 2. Design the logic of the solution.

A PRINT statement should be used to prompt the user to enter data. Because the data is being supplied by a person at the terminal, the INPUT statement will be used to enter data into the program. The pay will be calculated by taking the rate times the number of hours worked. A PRINT statement will then be used to print out the results.

Step 3. Code the program.

```
CLS
PRINT "ENTER RATE AND HOURS WORKED."
INPUT RATE, HOURS
LET PAY = RATE * HOURS
PRINT "RATE=";RATE,"HOURS=";HOURS,"PAY=";PAY
END
```

Step 4. Test and debug the program.

You are encouraged to enter this program into a computer and execute it with various sets of data. Before entering a program, you usually want to be sure that all of the old lines of code are erased from primary memory. Therefore, before you begin a new program, pull down the File menu (press Alt-F) and select ''New Program''. Then enter the QB statements and follow each statement by pressing the Enter key. Once the entire program is typed in, you can execute the program by pulling down the Run menu (Alt-R) and selecting ''Start''. Note the format (spacing) of the output resulting from this program.

Step 5. Document the program.

The full program, with REM statements, is as follows:

```
REM  COMPANY XYZ
REM  PAYROLL PROGRAM
REM  CREATED BY D. LENZ
REM  INPUT IS NUMBER OF HOURS WORKED AND RATE
REM  OUTPUT IS RATE, HOURS AND PAY FOR THE WEEK
PRINT  "ENTER RATE AND HOURS WORKED."
INPUT  RATE, HOURS
LET PAY = RATE * HOURS
PRINT "RATE=";RATE,"HOURS=";HOURS,"PAY=";PAY
END
```

Further Notes on This First Program:

1. The program would run for only one employee, and then end. To do the calculations for a second employee, you would need to execute the program a second time. Later, you will see how a repetition structure can be used to do the calculations for a group of employees with only one execution of the program.
2. In QB, prompts are allowed in INPUT statements. In other words, the PRINT and INPUT statements could have been written as the single statement

```
INPUT "ENTER RATE AND HOURS WORKED."; RATE,HOURS
```

3. The INPUT statement itself gives the user a prompt, namely a question mark, when data are to be entered. Thus, a sample execution of this program results in the following output:

```
ENTER RATE AND HOURS WORKED.
? 6.30, 41
RATE = 6.3    HOURS = 41    PAY = 258.3
```

You may not be happy with the monetary values printed above as 6.3 and 258.3. In Chapter Six, you will learn how to format currency output so that $6.30 and $258.30 would be displayed.

I. EXTENDING THE FIRST PROGRAM

The IF...THEN Statement

The IF...THEN statement allows a conditional transfer of flow in a program based on whether or not a condition specified in the logical expression (the "IF part") is true or false. The general format for the IF...THEN statement is

IF expression THEN conclusion

If the expression is true, the conclusion (the "THEN part") is executed; if it is false, program flow simply proceeds to the next line after the IF...THEN statement. The expressions are constructed using the relational operators described in section C. Consider the following example.

```
IF X > 0 THEN PRINT "X IS POSITIVE"
```

The sentence X IS POSITIVE will or will not be printed, depending on the value of X when this line is encountered. If X is greater than 0, the sentence is printed; if X is less than or equal to 0, the computer simply proceeds to the next executable statement in the program.

The conclusion in an IF...THEN statement can take forms other than a PRINT statement. For example, you can write

```
IF X + Y < 100 THEN LET A = 1
```

or

```
IF RESPONSE$ = "YES" THEN INPUT VALUE
```

You need only keep in mind that in an IF...THEN statement the conclusion is processed if and only if the logical expression is true.

Extending Program 1

You have now seen enough QuickBASIC statements to enable you to write a more powerful version of Program 1 to include pay for overtime hours.

Program 2.

Step 1. Describe the problem.

Company XYZ wants to update its payroll program to include overtime pay at "time and a half". More precisely, for hours worked over a base of 40 hours, the company will pay 1.5 times the hourly rate for the employee. The pay rate and the number of hours worked for each employee will be entered at the terminal. The output should consist of the rate, hours worked, and total pay for that individual.

Step 2. Design the logic of the solution.

The logic is much like that of Program 1 (you should review this now) except for the way pay is calculated. There are two methods for calculating pay in this program, depending on whether or not the employee has worked overtime hours. The program uses an IF...THEN statement, with the logical expression HOURS <= 40, to calculate pay when no overtime hours are worked. It uses an IF...THEN statement with the logical expression HOURS > 40 to calculate pay when overtime hours are worked. Note that the two expressions HOURS <= 40 and HOURS > 40 are never both true, and thus PAY will never be calculated more than once for a given input of RATE and HOURS.

Step 3. Code the program.

```
REM  COMPANY XYZ.
REM  PAYROLL PROGRAM WITH OVERTIME.
REM  CREATED BY R. ADAMS
REM  INPUT IS NUMBER OF HOURS WORKED AND RATE.
REM  OUTPUT IS RATE, HOURS AND PAY FOR THE WEEK.
PRINT "ENTER RATE AND HOURS WORKED."
INPUT RATE, HOURS
IF HOURS <= 40 THEN PAY = RATE * HOURS
IF HOURS > 40 THEN PAY = 40 * RATE + 1.5 * RATE * (HOURS - 40)
PRINT "RATE=";RATE,"HOURS=";HOURS,"PAY=";PAY
END
```

Step 4. Test and debug the program.

As an exercise, test the program by entering it into your computer and executing it with various sets of data. A good set of test data would include the value 40 for HOURS in order to determine if this “boundary condition” is handled correctly. In this case you would be checking if the = sign is in the correct place in line 80 rather than in line 90. (Would it make a difference here?)

In future programs Step 4 will not be mentioned explicitly, but often a test (a run) of the program will be included following the listing.

Step 5. Document the program.

To avoid repeating lines of code twice, as was done in Steps 3 and 5 of Program 1, the REM statements were included in the listing of the code in Step 3 here. For future programs, Step 5 will be incorporated directly into Step 3.

Further Notes on Program 2:

1. In Chapter Two you will see how the two IF statements in this program can be combined into a single IF...THEN...ELSE structure.
2. The following types of statements are used in Program 2:

   (a) those that give general information (the first and third REM statements)

(b) those that indicate what the program is to accomplish (the second, fourth, and fifth REM statements)

(c) those that initialize or assign (the INPUT and the conclusion of the IF statements)

(d) those that indicate a calculation to be performed (the assignment to PAY in the IF statements)

(e) a conditional branch (the IF statements)

(f) those that give output (the PRINT statements)

(g) the one that terminates the program (the END statement)

J. REVIEW EXERCISES

1. Decide if the following are valid or invalid variable names in QuickBASIC. If valid, write the word "valid"; if invalid, change the name to make it valid.

   (a) R1
   (b) PAY
   (c) "TEST"
   (d) 1A
   (e) TOTAL COST
   (f) NAME$
   (g) T1$

2. Determine the value of X after each of the following is executed. (Consider each lettered problem independently).

   (a) LET X = 3 + 2 * 5 / 10

   (b) LET X = 6 * 2 ^ 3

   (c) LET X = (6 * 2) ^ 3

   (d) LET X = 9 ^ 1 / 2

   (e) LET X = 9 ^ (1 / 2)

   (f) LET X = 9 - 4 * 2
   LET X = 7 + 6 + 8 / 2

3. Explain the differences among GRADE, GRADE$, and "GRADE" when used in a QuickBASIC program.

4. If A = 1, B = 2, and C = 3, which of the following logical expressions are true?

   (a) A + B >= C
   (b) A < > B
   (c) A + B + C > 10

5. Correct the following program so that it performs as the REM statements indicate.

```
REM  PROGRAM TO DETERMINE WHETHER THE FIRST OR
REM  THE SECOND NUMBER ENTERED IS LARGER.
PRINT "ENTER TWO UNEQUAL NUMBERS."
INPUT X, Y
IF X < Y THEN PRINT "THE FIRST NUMBER IS LARGER."
IF X > Y THEN PRINT "THE SECOND NUMBER IS LARGER."
END
```

6. Show the output for each of the following programs.

(a)

```
LET A = 4
LET B = 3
LET C = 2 ^ B / A
IF C > 10 THEN LET C = 100
IF C < 2 THEN LET C = 0
PRINT C
END
```

(b)

```
LET A = 5
LET B = 3
LET C = B * A / 30
IF C > 0 THEN LET C = 10
IF C > 8 THEN LET C = 4
IF C * A > 10 THEN LET C = 1
PRINT C
END
```

K. LAB EXERCISES

1. Enter the following QuickBASIC program.

```
REM MY FIRST PROGRAM
PRINT "THIS IS EASY."
END
```

Once the program is typed in, you'll want the computer to execute the program (carry out the instructions). Pull down the Run menu and select ''Start''.

What was the output (the response from the computer)? If you see an error message, check your typing with the above.

____

Notice that the computer is waiting for another QB command. You can now edit the program. Replace the first two lines with

```
REM MY SECOND PROGRAM
PRINT "HI TO EVERYONE"
```

The computer is waiting for the next command. Pull down the Run menu and select ''Start''.

What is the output? THIS IS EASY
HI TO EVERYONE

Why didn't the computer print THIS IS EASY?
It did

How did the computer "know" what program to execute?
?

What happened to the original version of the program?
?

What is displayed now?
THIS IS EASY
HI TO EVERYONE

Edit your program to look like the listing below. Enter your own name for <your name>.

```
REM   MY FIRST QUICKBASIC PROGRAM
REM   <your name>
REM   DATE: (date the program was completed)
REM   PURPOSE: (description of the program)
PRINT "THIS IS EASY."
END
```

Finally, save this program. Pull down the File menu and select "Save As". When the dialog box opens, type in the filename FIRST and press the Enter key.

What message is displayed?
File already exists. Overwrite?

To exit QB, pull down the File menu and select "Quit".

2. Enter the following program.

```
CLS
PRINT "ENTER A VALUE FOR X."
INPUT X
LET A = 625 * X
PRINT A
END
```

Run the program to determine the output for the following values of X. Enter the value shown after the question mark.

?10
output 6250

?14.678
output 9173.75

?.000000567
output 3.5437 E-04 normal notation .00035437

Why is this in E notation? ______

?-.00000067
Output -41875 normal notation ______

? (For this execution just hit the Enter key)
output ______

Judging by the output, what value does the computer assign to X? ______

3. Enter the following program into your computer:

```
CLS
REM PROGRAM TO ADD TWO NUMBERS ENTERED AT THE TERMINAL
PRINT "PLEASE ENTER 2 NUMBERS TO BE ADDED."
INPUT A, B
PRINT "SUM IS"; A + B
END
```

Run the program three times, doing the following: in response to the INPUT statement, enter the values shown below and document how the computer handles these three situations in the corresponding blanks.

(a) 5, 3 Sum IS 8
(b) 5, 3, 9 Redo From Start
(c) 5 REDO FROM START

4. Enter the following lines of code into your computer:

```
INPUT X
PRINT X
```

In response to the INPUT statement, enter 100. What is the computer's output?

______

In response to the INPUT statement, enter BOB. What is the computer's output?

______

5. Enter the following lines of code into your computer:

```
INPUT A$
PRINT A$
```

In response to the INPUT statement enter ''BOB''. What is the computer's output?

____

Run this program, entering the number 5 in response to the INPUT statement. How does the computer respond to this situation? (Keep in mind that you are entering the character string ''5'' and not the number 5.)

____

L. PROGRAMMING PROBLEMS

Follow the five steps outlined in this chapter when writing the following programs.

1. Write a single QB program to
   (a) print the numbers 1 through 10 vertically, and
   (b) print the numbers 1 through 10 horizontally.
2. Write a QB program to calculate the number of hours a person has lived. The input to the program will be the age of the person in years (you can be as precise as you wish here). The output will be the number of hours lived.
3. In 1627, the Indians sold Manhattan Island for $24.00. If they had invested this money at 8% interest compounded annually, what would this investment be worth in 1991? Write a QB program to determine the answer. In your program, use the formula

$$A = P * (1 + I) \wedge N$$

where

A = current value of the investment,
P = principal,
I = interest rate,
N = number of years.

4. Modify the program you wrote for number 3 above so that the user can input any interest rate at the terminal. Run the program for I = 5% and I = 10%. Compare the results.
5. One standard use of the IF...THEN statement is to check entered data to see if they meet required specifications. In fact, this was done in Review Exercise 5 when the numbers entered were checked for equality. Write a program to compute the area of a square (AREA = SIDELENGTH ^ 2) where the length of the square is entered at the terminal. Use an IF...THEN statement to check if the length entered is non-negative. If the length entered is negative, give the user another opportunity (as you did in Review Exercise 5) to enter the side length. Print out the calculated area.

CHAPTER TWO

PROGRAM CONTROL STRUCTURES

"*Luck is the residue of design.*" (Branch Rickey, former professional baseball general manager)

A. INTRODUCTION

A programmer may write a program to accomplish a particular task without being overly concerned with the structure and readability of the work. The resulting lines of code may contain such an intricate maze of statements that even the original programmer may have trouble understanding the logic of the program.

The alternative to writing programs in such an unstructured manner is to follow a modular approach using program control structures in designing programs. The modular approach allows you to divide a relatively large programming task into smaller units that can be developed more easily. A structured program design generally helps reduce programming errors and the time spent on debugging and maintaining the program.

A well-designed program is conceptualized as a combination of programming control structures. Furthermore, one principle of a structured programming approach is that any program can be represented by sequence, selection, and repetition control structures. These three fundamental programming structures are presented in this chapter.

B. FLOWCHARTS

Recall that in the second step of the programming process that we discussed in the last chapter, the programmer designs the general logic of the solution. It is here that the logical sequence of statements for a program is developed. As an aid in design (as well as in documentation) a programmer can use a design technique known as a *flowchart*. Flowcharts depict QuickBASIC statements and program flow by interconnecting special flowchart symbols with flow lines. The symbols indicate the type of operation to be performed. The most common flowchart symbols and their meanings are shown in Figure 2.1.

Symbol	Geometric Shape	Meaning
	Rectangle	One or more processing steps
	Parallelogram	Generalized input to or output from the system
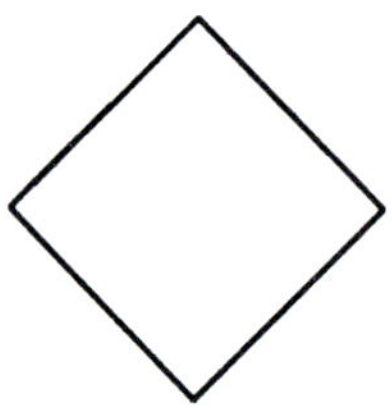	Diamond	Decision step (i.e., a point in a program where one of several branches through the code may be taken)
	Hexagon	Preparation step, such as dimensioning an array (see Chapter Four)
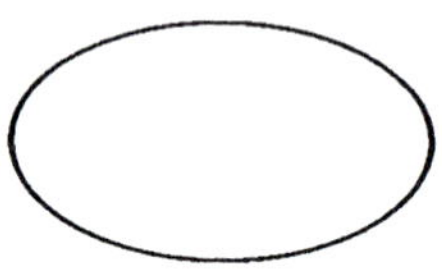	Oval	Terminal symbol indicating the beginning or end of the program

Figure 2.1. Common Flowchart Symbols

The flowchart in Figure 2.2 depicts the steps in Program 1, the payroll program, from the last chapter. Notice how the symbols correspond to the meaning of the QB statements and how they are shown in logical order connected by flow lines. The oval start symbol represents the beginning of the program. REM statements are non-executable and therefore are not represented in the flowchart. The first parallelogram represents output corresponding to the first PRINT statement in the program. The next parallelogram corresponds to the input of the rate and hours. The assignment statement where the calculation is done is represented by a rectangle. The last PRINT statement is depicted by another parallelogram, and the END statement is represented by the terminal symbol.

Flowcharting, when used as a design technique, precedes the writing of lines of code for a program. Note that the hard work of developing the logic of a program is completed once the flowchart is drawn, and thus it is a relatively simple task to proceed from a flowchart to specific lines of code for a program.

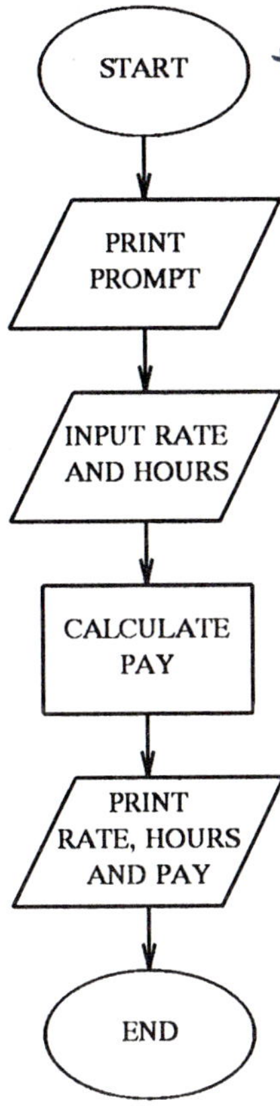

Figure 2.2. Flowchart for Program 1

C. FUNDAMENTAL CONTROL STRUCTURES

Sets of statements in a program (or, in fact, the program as a whole) can be classified as one of three fundamental programming structures: sequence, selection, or repetition. In a *sequence structure*, the processing steps are simply executed in sequence, one after another, as depicted in Figure 2.3a. In a *selection structure*, a decision is made, and based on that decision only one of two or more sequences of code is executed (Figure 2.3b). The decision statement is often a conditional (IF...THEN) statement. It may be the case that one of the two rectangles in Figure 2.3b is empty and thus, if the condition is true, something is done in the program; if it is false, nothing is done, or vice versa (for example, see Figure 2.4). A *repetition structure*, also called a loop, is depicted in Figure 2.3c. In this figure, the rectangle represents a set of statements that will be executed repeatedly as long as the conditional represented by the diamond sends program execution down that path. When a certain condition is met, the conditional changes value, and the loop is exited via the path on the right side of Figure 2.3c. The FOR/NEXT and the WHILE/WEND QB statement pairs are used to construct all of the repetition structures in the programs presented in this text.

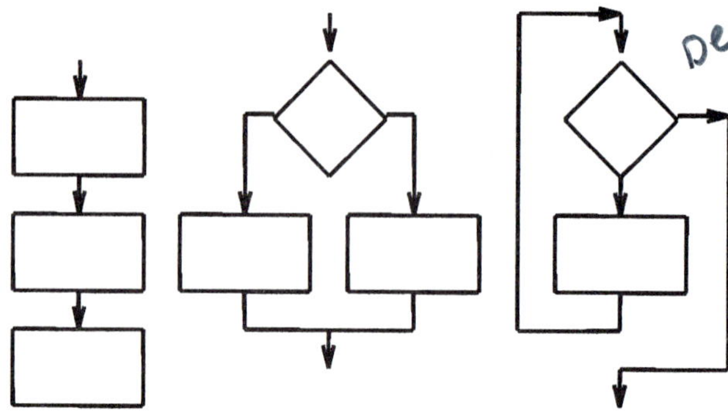

(a) Sequence   (b) Selection   (c) Repetition

Figure 2.3. Programming Structures

Figure 2.4 displays the flowchart for Program 2, the payroll program with overtime. Note how the selection structures are depicted in this diagram. If a condition is true, then a calculation is performed; if it is false, no calculation is performed and control simply passes to the next executable statement in the program. You should carefully observe that the program flow corresponds to the flow lines in Figure 2.4. Note that this flowchart contains a sequence and two selection structures, but no repetition structures.

How can you, as a beginning programmer, use these control structures to your advantage when writing a program? A new programmer, when given a large program to write, will often try to write it from start to finish as one entity, which may be a formidable task. A more reasonable approach is to divide the large problem into smaller tasks or *modules* that can be developed relatively easily. These modules generally represent the logical parts of the program, which consist of a combination of sequence, selection, and repetition structures. For example, in a corporate setting, Program 2 might contain many more details and many more lines of code. Then modules could be developed for inputting values, calculating pay without overtime, calculating pay with overtime, and outputting results. These major modules (concepts) correspond to parts of the flowchart in Figure 2.4. Once the modules are completed, the programmer incorporates them in the appropriate sequence into a single program. In this way the modular approach can reduce the complexity of the programming task.

D. REPETITION STRUCTURES

Repetition structures, also known as loops, are used when a sequence of statements needs to be repeated in a program. The programmer decides which instructions are to be repeated and, if possible, how many times the repetition is to take place. In this section, loops will be exhibited in programs using one of the following sets of statements:

FOR/NEXT pair of statements,

WHILE/WEND pair of statements.

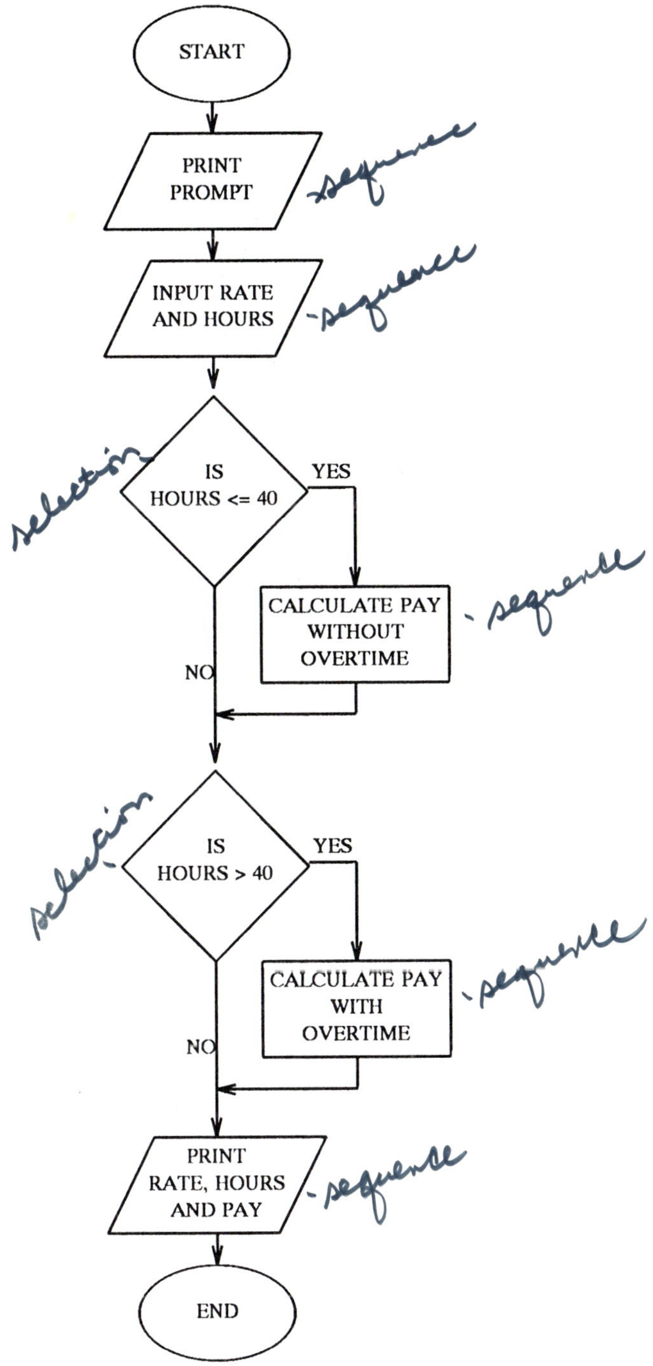

Figure 2.4. Flowchart for Program 2

FOR/NEXT Repetition Structures

The need to control looping occurs so often in programming that a formal structure has been developed in QuickBASIC to do this job. The FOR and NEXT statements create a concise loop in which all of the statements between FOR and NEXT are executed repeatedly. The general form of the FOR/NEXT loop is as follows:

FOR index variable = initial value TO limit value STEP increment value

statement(s) to be repeated

NEXT index variable

Examples of this structure include

(1)
```
FOR I = 1 TO 10 STEP 1
.
.
.
NEXT I
```

and

(2)
```
FOR T = 1 TO 25 STEP 2
.
.
.
NEXT T
```

and

(3)
```
FOR J = 10 TO 1 STEP -1
.
.
.
NEXT J
```

The execution of a FOR/NEXT loop begins by setting the index variable to the initial value. This value is tested against the limit value to determine if the body of the loop should be executed. If the loop is traversed, the NEXT statement is encountered, which loops control back to the FOR statement, at which time the value of the index variable is increased by the increment value and then tested again against the limit value. Once the value of the variable surpasses the limit value (is greater than the limit value when the step is positive or less than the limit value when the step is negative), control transfers to the statement immediately following the NEXT statement. In the above examples, the index variable takes on the following values on successive traversals of the loop:

(1) I = 1, 2, 3, 4, 5, 6, 7, 8, 9, 10, 11. Note that when I takes on the value of 11, the limit value of 10 is exceeded and the loop is terminated. This loop is traversed 10

times, with I taking on the values 1, 2, 3...10.

(2) T = 1, 3, 5, 7, 9, 11, 13, 15, 17, 19, 21, 23, 25, 27. When T reaches 27, the limit value 25 is exceeded and the loop is terminated. This loop is executed 13 times.

(3) J = 10, 9, 8, 7, 6, 5, 4, 3, 2, 1, 0. When J becomes 0, J finally "passes" the limit value of 1. This loop is executed 10 times. Examples will be presented that demonstrate how a negative increment in a FOR statement can be very useful. (See Chapter Four.)

Consider the following program:

Program 3.

Step 1. Describe the problem.

Write a program that doubles, triples, and quadruples each number in the set of integers from 1 to 10 inclusive. The numbers 1 through 10 will be generated in the program (not input from a terminal). The output will consist of the original numbers and their required multiples in a column format.

Step 2. Design the logic of the solution.

The program should set the index variable N to the initial value of 1 and print out N, 2*N, 3*N and 4*N. Using an incremental value of 1, it should continue this process through the limit value of 10 for N.

Step 3. Code the program.

```
REM  THIS PROGRAM DOUBLES, TRIPLES AND
REM  QUADRUPLES EACH NUMBER IN THE SET
REM  OF NUMBERS FROM 1 TO 10.
PRINT "N", "N DOUBLED", "N TRIPLED", "N QUADRUPLED"
PRINT
FOR N = 1 TO 10 STEP 1
   PRINT N, 2*N, 3*N, 4*N
NEXT N
END
```

The output is as follows:

N	N DOUBLED	N TRIPLED	N QUADRUPLED
1	2	3	4
2	4	6	8
3	6	9	12
4	8	12	16
5	10	15	20
6	12	18	24
7	14	21	28
8	16	24	32
9	18	27	36
10	20	30	40

Further Notes on Program 3:

1. The first PRINT statement prints a heading for each of the four columns, one title in each of the first four print zones.
2. Using PRINT with no variables or constants listed results in the blank line between the headings and the numerical display.
3. The numbers appear left justified, one space to the right of "N" in each column. The initial space is available for the minus sign, which would accompany a negative number. No sign appears if the number is positive or zero.
4. The flowchart for this program is shown below in Figure 2.5. You are encouraged to compare the flow in the diagram with the statements in the program listing, paying special attention to the looping structure. Note that the FOR/NEXT statements accomplish the tasks of initializing, testing, and incrementing the index variable N.
5. The PRINT statement inside the loop is indented because the readability of a program is enhanced if the body of a FOR/NEXT loop is indented. This formatting convention helps convey the structure of the program to the reader.

Other Comments on FOR/NEXT statements:

1. The initial, limit, and increment values can be either constants, variables, or arithmetic expressions. For example, the following are valid FOR statements:

```
FOR I = J TO 100 STEP 3
FOR K = 4 TO 10 STEP T
FOR I = 1 TO J - 3 STEP 2
```

2. If the step size is 1, the STEP clause can be omitted from the FOR statement. In other words, the FOR statement in Program 3 could have been written as the equivalent statement

```
40 FOR N = 1 TO 10
```

3. FOR and NEXT statements must occur in pairs, using the same index variable.
4. Some versions of BASIC do not allow the initial, limit, and increment values to be altered within the body of the loop. Even if this is possible, it is not a good programming practice to do so, because such changes can lead to error-prone programming. For example, in Program 3 suppose the variable TOP has an initial value of 2, the FOR statement is FOR N = 1 TO TOP STEP 1, and the loop contains a statement TOP = TOP + 1. This program in theory would run forever because N would never reach the limit value, which would be increasing by 1 each time through the loop.
5. The value of the index variable should not be modified by statements within the loop.
6. Entry into a loop must be made by executing the FOR statement.

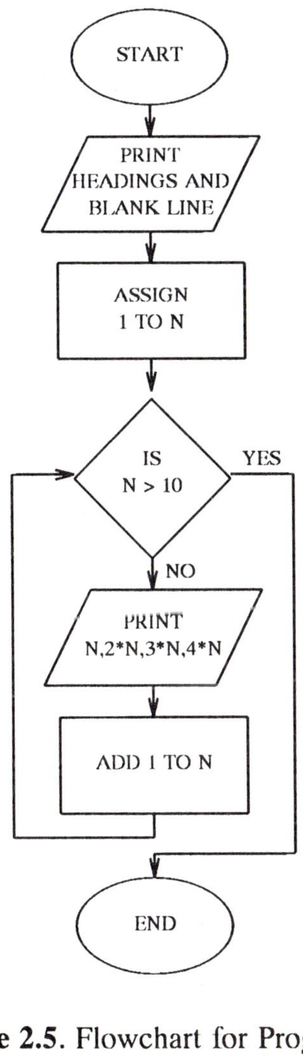

Figure 2.5. Flowchart for Program 3

Consider the next program, which shows the common application of finding the largest value in a set of numbers. This program could be enhanced for the purpose of finding the salesperson with the highest sales for a given month, the student with the highest grade point average, or the elementary school child with the most boxes of cookies sold in a fund-raising drive.

<u>Program 4.</u>

<u>Step 1.</u> Describe the problem.

Write a program that will find the largest number in a set of 20 numbers entered at a terminal. The output should be simply the largest number.

<u>Step 2.</u> Design the logic of the solution.

Assign the first value entered into the variable LARGE. This variable will be used to hold the largest value throughout the program. (With only one value entered, this value must be the largest and therefore it makes sense to assign it to LARGE outside the loop.) Because the next value will be the second one entered, the loop starts with an initial value of 2. As each new number is assigned to the variable VALUE, compare VALUE to LARGE. If VALUE is greater than LARGE, assign VALUE to LARGE (i.e., VALUE is the new largest number), but if VALUE is less than or equal to LARGE, do nothing at all, which will retain the previous value of LARGE as the largest. Each time through the loop, after the appropriate value of LARGE is established, the index variable I is incremented by 1 and checked against the limit value of 20. Finally, after 20 values have been entered, print out the largest number.

<u>Step 3.</u> Code the program.

```
REM  PROGRAM TO FIND LARGEST NUMBER IN A SET OF
REM  20 NUMBERS.
PRINT "ENTER FIRST NUMBER."
REM  FIRST NUMBER ENTERED IS LARGEST SO FAR, PUT IT
REM  IN LARGE.
INPUT LARGE
FOR I = 2 TO 20
  PRINT "ENTER NEXT NUMBER."
  INPUT VALUE
  IF VALUE > LARGE THEN LARGE = VALUE
NEXT I
PRINT "LARGEST IS"; LARGE
END
```

Further Notes on Program 4:

1. The statements within the loop are indented to make it easy to identify the repetition structure in the program.
2. You should be convinced that the conclusion in the IF statement could *not* be written

   VALUE = LARGE

   What would be the result in this case?
3. The word LET in the conclusion of the IF statement was omitted. As mentioned in Chapter One, this option is available in QuickBASIC.

   The flowchart for Program 4 is left as an exercise for you.

The next two programs use the FOR/NEXT repetition structure and the standard step-by-step approach.

Program 5.

Step 1. Describe the problem.

Calculate the average of 15 numbers that are to be entered from the terminal. Output the average with an appropriate message.

Step 2. Design the logic of the solution.

Since a particular action (entering a number) is to be repeated 15 times, a FOR/NEXT loop is appropriate. The program should initialize SUM to 0 before the loop, add the numbers to SUM within the loop, and then calculate the average and output the results after the loop.

Step 3. Code the program.

```
REM  PROGRAM TO CALCULATE AVERAGE OF 15 NUMBERS
SUM = 0
FOR I = 1 TO 15
  PRINT "ENTER A NUMBER"
  INPUT NUMBER
  SUM = SUM + NUMBER
NEXT I
AVE = SUM / 15
PRINT "THE AVERAGE IS"; AVE
END
```

Further Notes on Program 5:

1. Switching the statement initializing the variable SUM and the FOR statement would have disastrous consequences for this program. (Why?)
2. You are encouraged to insert just before NEXT I the statement shown below to see the accumulation of the sum of the numbers in the variable SUM.

   ```
   PRINT SUM
   ```

3. This program calculates the average of a known number of scores. In a later program (Program 7) the average of an unknown number of scores will be calculated.

Program 6.

Step 1. Describe the problem.

Calculate the product of the odd integers from 1 to 15 inclusive and print out the result.

Step 2. Design the logic of the solution.

You must process a set of numbers and calculate a "cumulative" product as you proceed. This suggests the use of a FOR/NEXT loop. However, since only the odd integers 1, 3, 5, 7, 9, 11, 13, 15 are to be used in the calculations, you can skip the even numbers by using an increment of 2 in the FOR statement. If the variable PRODUCT holds the product, then PRODUCT must be initialized to 1. (Why?) Then an initial value of 3 can be used in the FOR statement.

Step 3. Code the program.

```
REM  PROGRAM THAT CALCULATES PRODUCT OF ALL
REM  ODD INTEGERS FROM 1 TO 15.
LET PRODUCT = 1
FOR I = 3 TO 15 STEP 2
  LET PRODUCT = PRODUCT * I
NEXT I
PRINT "PRODUCT IS"; PRODUCT
END
```

The output is as follows:

```
PRODUCT IS 2027025
```

WHILE/WEND Repetition Structures

The WHILE and WHILE END (abbreviated WEND) statements are another common way to set up a looping structure in BASIC. Many times repetition is performed not a prescribed number of times (as in a FOR statement), but rather *while* a certain condition holds. For example, you make payments on a loan while the balance is not 0, a computer operator may continue to process data while more values need to be entered, and an usher in a theater of 500 seats may continue to seat people while seats are available. The general form of the WHILE/WEND loop is as follows:

```
WHILE logical expression
  }
  }  statements to be repeated
  }
WEND
```

Examples of this structure include

```
(1)                 WHILE BALANCE < > 0
                         .
                         .
                         .
                    WEND
```

and

```
(2)                 WHILE SEATS < = 500
                         .
                         .
                         .
                    WEND
```

If the expression in the WHILE statement is true, the statements in the loop are executed until WEND is reached. When WEND is encountered, the computer branches back to the WHILE statement and the expression is checked again. As soon as the expression is false, the looping is stopped and the next statement following WEND is executed. Unlike the FOR statement, the variable in the expression in the WHILE statement is not automatically incremented. Therefore there must be a statement inside the loop that changes the value of a variable in the expression.

The following example uses the WHILE/WEND structure as well as a trailer. A *trailer*, also called a dummy value, is entered after all of the actual data for the program have been processed. If the trailer is entered, control is transferred out of the loop, whereas if an actual data value is entered, looping continues. You should always pick a trailer that cannot be confused with the actual data in the program.

Program 7.

Step 1. Describe the problem.

A teacher wishes to average a large (and unknown) number of test scores, where the scores can range from 0 to 100. The scores are entered from the terminal and the desired output is simply the average.

Step 2. Design the logic of the solution.

Instead of taking the time to count the number of scores, the teacher can choose to follow the last real score entered into the program with a trailer. The trailer -1, which is outside the range of scores 0 to 100, is chosen here. The first step is to initialize a summing variable SUM and a counting variable COUNT to 0. COUNT will keep track of the number of scores entered. When a number is entered, determine if it is the trailer -1. If it is -1, all real values have been entered and thus the program can proceed to the statement where the average is calculated. If the number entered is not the trailer, then the sum and count are incremented and looping continues. Upon termination of the looping process, the average is calculated and printed.

Step 3. Code the program.

```
REM -1 IS USED AS A TRAILER
SUM = 0
COUNT = 0
PRINT "ENTER A NUMBER."
INPUT SCORE
WHILE SCORE < > -1
  SUM = SUM + SCORE
  COUNT = COUNT + 1
  PRINT "ENTER A NUMBER (-1 TO END)."
  INPUT SCORE
WEND
AVE = SUM / COUNT
PRINT "THE AVERAGE IS";AVE
END
```

Further Notes on Program 7:

1. In most versions of BASIC, variables are initialized to 0. Therefore the second and third statements are really unnecessary. So why are they included here? It is a good programming practice to initialize all summing variables to 0. Most other languages do not initialize variables to 0, and in those cases you must remember to include such lines. Therefore it is a good habit to always include the initialization of summing variables.
2. Notice that the second INPUT SCORE statement must be placed after the statements incrementing the SUM and COUNT variables. This latest value of SCORE is then available to be used in the logical expression in the WHILE statement.
3. The reader should consider what happens if the first number entered is -1. What error message will appear?

Nested Loops

FOR/NEXT and WHILE/WEND loops can be nested (one inside another). Each of the nested FOR/NEXT loops must use a different index variable and must be entirely contained within the next outer loop. For example, the following is a valid structure

```
FOR I = 1 TO 5
  FOR J = 1 TO 5
    .
    .
    .
  NEXT J
NEXT I
```

whereas the next examples are not valid:

```
FOR I = 1 TO 5
   FOR J = 1 TO 3
      .
      .
      .
NEXT I
   NEXT J
```

```
FOR I = 1 TO 5
   FOR I = 1 TO 3
      .
      .
      .
NEXT I
   NEXT I
```

Note the output from the following program 8A:

Program 8A.

```
REM  NESTED LOOPS
FOR I = 1 TO 5
  FOR J = 1 TO 3
    PRINT I; " "; J
  NEXT J
NEXT I
END
```

Output:

```
1  1
1  2
1  3
2  1
2  2
2  3
3  1
3  2
3  3
4  1
4  2
4  3
5  1
5  2
5  3
```

Notes on Program 8A:

1. The PRINT statement is executed 15 times.

2. The statement within the inner loop is "doubly indented".
3. When I is fixed at any single value, J takes on the values 1, 2, 3 and 4. When J becomes 4, the inner loop is terminated and control passes to the next statement after the inner loop, namely NEXT I. Then I is incremented and when the outer loop is traversed again, the inner loop index J is reinitialized to 1.
4. The space is used in the PRINT statement to give the output the appearance of two separate numbers rather than one two-digit number.
5. The equivalent program, Program 8B, using WHILE/WEND loops is given below. Note that when the number of traversals through the loop is known, the FOR/NEXT structure is easier to follow.

Program 8B.

```
REM  NESTED WHILE LOOPS
I = 1
WHILE I <= 5
   J = 1
   WHILE J <= 3
      J = J + 1
      PRINT I; " "; J
   WEND
   I = I + 1
WEND
END
```

In the next program, note how a nested loop is employed to develop numerical output in tabular form.

Program 9.

Step 1. Describe the problem.

Suppose you are planning to apply for a loan to buy an automobile. You will want to know the monthly payment for various loan amounts coupled with various interest rates. The problem is to produce a table displaying your payment options.

Step 2. Design the logic of the solution.

The output is to contain a table with rows corresponding to loan amounts and columns corresponding to various interest rates. For each loan amount, you'll want to display the monthly payment at various interest rates. This suggests an outer loop where the index variable corresponds to varying loan amounts and an inner loop controlling the interest rates. The user will be able to choose the first (lowest) loan amount and the first (lowest) interest rate contained in the table. The equation to calculate the monthly payment is

$$PAYMENT = LOAN * I/(1-(1+I)^{-N})$$

where

N = number of monthly payments
I = monthly interest rate (annual rate / 12)

<u>Step 3.</u> Code the program.

```
' THIS PROGRAM COMPUTES THE MONTHLY PAYMENT TO PAY OFF
' VARIOUS LOAN AMOUNTS BEGINNING WITH AN AMOUNT DETERMINED
' BY THE VARIABLE FIRSTLOAN.  VARIOUS INTEREST RATES ARE
' CONSIDERED, BEGINNING WITH A RATE GIVEN BY THE VARIABLE
' FIRSTRATE.  THE LENGTH OF THE LOAN IS DETERMINED BY THE
' VARIABLE TERM.  VALUES FOR THE VARIABLES FIRSTLOAN,
' FIRSTRATE, AND TERM WILL BE ENTERED BY THE USER.

' ************* INPUT SECTION OF THE PROGRAM *************
CLS
PRINT "ENTER THE FIRST LOAN AMOUNT TO CONSIDER"
INPUT FIRSTLOAN
LASTLOAN = FIRSTLOAN + 5000
PRINT "ENTER THE FIRST ANNUAL INTEREST RATE TO CONSIDER"
INPUT FIRSTRATE
LASTRATE = FIRSTRATE + 4
PRINT "ENTER THE NUMBER OF MONTHLY PAYMENTS FOR THE LOAN"
INPUT TERM

' ************** PRINT HEADINGS SECTION *****************
PRINT "MONTHLY PAYMENTS FOR VARIOUS";TERM;" MONTH LOANS"
PRINT
PRINT " LOAN";"              ";"ANNUAL INTEREST RATES"
PRINT "AMOUNT    ";
FOR RATE = FIRSTRATE TO LASTRATE
   PRINT RATE;"      ";
NEXT RATE
PRINT

' ************* BODY OF THE TABLE SECTION **************
FOR LOAN = FIRSTLOAN TO LASTLOAN STEP 1000
   PRINT LOAN;
   FOR RATE = FIRSTRATE TO LASTRATE
      MONRATE = RATE/1200
      NUMERATOR = LOAN * MONRATE
      DENOMINATOR = 1 - (1 + MONRATE) ^ (-TERM)
      PAYMENT = NUMERATOR / DENOMINATOR
      PRINT PAYMENT;
   NEXT RATE
   PRINT
NEXT LOAN
END
```

Sample Output:

```
ENTER THE FIRST LOAN AMOUNT TO CONSIDER
? 11500
ENTER THE FIRST ANNUAL INTEREST RATE TO CONSIDER
? 8
ENTER THE NUMBER OF MONTHLY PAYMENTS FOR THE LOAN
? 48

MONTHLY PAYMENTS FOR VARIOUS 48 MONTH LOANS
```

LOAN	ANNUAL INTEREST RATES				
AMOUNT	8	9	10	11	12
11500	280.7486	286.178	291.6697	297.2235	302.8391
12500	305.1615	311.063	317.0323	323.069	329.1729
13500	329.5744	335.9481	342.3949	348.9145	355.5068
14500	353.9874	360.8331	367.7574	374.76	381.8406
15500	378.4003	385.7182	393.1201	400.6056	408.1745
16500	402.8132	410.6032	418.4826	426.4511	434.5083

Further Notes on Program 9:

1. The alternative to REM, namely the apostrophe, is used to indicate remark statements in this program. Notice also the use of remarks to help identify important sections in the program.
2. The semicolon at the end of the statements PRINT "AMOUNT " and PRINT RATE;" "; are used as a formatting technique to print "AMOUNT" and the interest rates on one line. The spaces in these statements are used to display the output in a more precise way than simply using print fields.
3. The last loan amount considered can be easily changed by revising the statement LASTLOAN = FIRSTLOAN + 5000. What line would you change to alter the increment in the loan values displayed?
4. Note that an annual interest rate is entered as you would say the value (e.g., 9 for 9% or 9.5 for 9.5%). Therefore to establish a monthly rate in the statement MONRATE = RATE/1200, you need to divide by 100 to obtain a decimal representation (e.g., .09) as well as by 12 to obtain a monthly rate. Thus you see the denominator 1200.
5. The statements inside the nested loop are executed 30 times in a single run of this program.
6. The output of the payment amounts certainly needs additional formatting to round decimal values, align decimal points, and introduce dollar signs. These considerations will be addressed in Chapter Six when the PRINT USING statement is discussed.

The READ/DATA Statements

Up to now, you have learned of two ways to enter data into a program, namely, through the use of the LET and INPUT statements. The LET or assignment statement is appropriate when initialization of a variable is needed. The INPUT statement is chosen when an interaction between the computer and the user of the program is desired. However, neither of these statements is very convenient if a great amount of data has to be entered into a program. In this situation, data can be read from online computer files, as you'll see in Chapter Seven, or the READ/DATA combination of statements can be used. The general form of these statements is

```
READ list of variables
    .
    .
    .
DATA constant values
```

The variables in the READ statement are assigned values from the DATA statement in the order in which they occur. Numeric and character string variables must be matched with constants of the appropriate data type. READ statements appear when the assignment of a value to a variable is required in the program. DATA statements can appear anywhere in a program but are generally grouped together just before the END statement. Consider the following examples:

(1)

```
READ X, Y, Z
    .
    .
    .
DATA 10, 20, 30
```

After the READ statement is executed, X = 10, Y = 20, and Z = 30.

(2)

```
READ X, Y, Z          READ X            READ X
   .                  READ Y            READ Y
   .                  READ Z            READ Z
   .                    .                 .
   .                    .                 .
   .                    .                 .
DATA 10               DATA 10
DATA 20               DATA 20           DATA 10, 20, 30
DATA 30               DATA 30
```

All three sets of code displayed above accomplish the same assignment of values to variables as the lines of code in example (1).

(3) READ A$, X, B$, Y

.
.
.

READ A, B

.
.
.

DATA "SMITH", 80, "ROBERTS", 90, 1, 2

.
.
.

After the first READ statement is executed, A$ = SMITH, X = 80, B$ = ROBERTS, and Y = 90. A pointer inside the computer keeps track of which data element is to be read next. Then, when the second READ statement is encountered, A is set to 1 and B is assigned the value 2.

(4) READ A, B, C

.
.
.

DATA 160, 200

When not enough data is supplied, the computer prints an error message. In this case, you would see the message

OUT OF DATA

(5) DATA 1, 7, 10
READ X, Y

As mentioned earlier, the DATA statements can be placed anywhere in the program. If no other READ statements appear in the program, then the value 10 in the DATA statement would simply be ignored.

Note that each item of data is separated by commas. String constants do not have to be placed in quotation marks unless a comma is part of the string. For example, the following DATA line contains two city and state locations.

DATA "CHICAGO,ILLINOIS", "MUNCIE,INDIANA"

If the quotation marks were omitted, then the DATA statement would contain four data items.

Program 10.

Step 1. Describe the problem.

A program is needed to calculate the volume of four rectangular boxes. The input is the length, width, and height of each box. The output is the volume of each box.

Step 2. Design the logic of the solution.

You can supply the data to the program through a READ/DATA combination of statements. A FOR/NEXT loop can be used to calculate a volume four times. The READ statement will of course be in the loop to assign to three variables the dimensions of each box.

Step 3. Code the program.

```
REM  VOLUME PROGRAM WITH LOOPING
FOR I = 1 TO 4
  READ LENGTH, WDTH, HEIGHT
  PRINT "VOLUME OF BOX"; I; "IS"; LENGTH*WDTH*HEIGHT
NEXT I
DATA 30, 5, 2, 6, 7, 5, 1, 4, 9.3, 11, 12, 4
END
```

The output would appear as follows:

```
VOLUME OF BOX 1 IS 300
VOLUME OF BOX 2 IS 210
VOLUME OF BOX 3 IS 37.2
VOLUME OF BOX 4 IS 528
```

The variable name WDTH is used instead of the more obvious choice WIDTH because WIDTH is a reserved word in QuickBASIC.

The RESTORE Statement

If you need to read a set of data values more than once in a program, you do not have to type in redundant DATA statements. Instead, you can use the RESTORE statement, which causes the pointer that points to the next data element to be repositioned at the first value in the first DATA statement in the program. The values in the DATA statements can then be read a second time. The RESTORE statement can be used as often as it is needed in a program.

The format for the RESTORE statement is

RESTORE

Some versions of BASIC allow the form

RESTORE label or line #

This statement has the effect of moving the pointer to the first data element on that line. If the statement specified by the label or line number is not a DATA statement, the pointer is set to the next data element in the program.

Note the output from the following short program, which uses the READ, DATA, and RESTORE statements.

Program 11.

```
REM  EXAMPLE USING RESTORE
READ A, B, C
RESTORE
READ D, E, F, G
PRINT A; B; C; D; E; F; G
DATA 10, 20, 30, 40, 50, 60, 70
END
```

Output:

```
10  20  30  10  20  30  40
```

Using DATA Elements to Control Loops

The next two programs show how the first or the last data element in the DATA statement can be used for a special purpose in a program. In Program 12, the first value in the DATA statement is used to establish the limit value in a FOR/NEXT loop. In Program 13, the last value in the DATA statement is used as a trailer. You are encouraged to study these programming techniques.

Program 12.

```
REM  PROGRAM TO FIND SUM OF NUMBERS IN A DATA
REM  STATEMENT NOT INCLUDING THE FIRST, WHICH INDICATES
REM  NUMBER OF VALUES LEFT IN THE DATA STATEMENT.
SUM = 0
READ LIMIT
FOR I = 1 TO LIMIT
  READ X
  SUM = SUM + X
NEXT I
PRINT "THE SUM IS"; SUM
DATA 6, 19, 25, 47, 81, 41, 23
END
```

Output:

```
THE SUM IS 236
```

Program 13.

```
REM  PROGRAM TO FIND THE AVERAGE OF NUMBERS IN A
REM  DATA STATEMENT EXCLUDING THE LAST, WHICH IS
REM  THE TRAILER 9999
SUM = 0
COUNT = 0
```

```
READ N
WHILE N < > 9999
  SUM = SUM + N
  COUNT = COUNT + 1
  READ N
WEND
AVE = SUM / COUNT
PRINT "THE AVERAGE IS"; AVE
DATA 86, 92, 75, 49, 100, 99, 80, 9999
END
```

Output:

```
THE AVERAGE IS 83
```

E. SELECTION STRUCTURES

You have already seen the IF...THEN statement as one means by which you can incorporate a selection structure to choose one of the sequences of code in a program. This section will present a continuation of the discussion of the IF...THEN statement as well as an introduction to the IF...THEN...ELSE and the SELECT CASE selection statements.

IF...THEN Statement With Compound Logical Expressions

Logical expressions were introduced in the discussion of the IF...THEN statement in Chapter One. Recall that in this statement the conclusion is executed only if the expression is true. Sometimes in programming, you want several conditions satisfied before a conclusion is executed. For example, a long distance telephone company sends a bill to a customer if the last billing to that customer has been at least 30 days ago and also if the charges for that customer's calls have reached $5.00 or more. If the variable DAYS represents the number of days since the last billing and the variable TOTAL represents the customer's total charges, then the above conditions can be stated by the logical expression

DAYS >= 30 AND TOTAL >= 5.

This expression can be used in an IF...THEN statement in a program to determine whether or not the CHARGE should be calculated. The BASIC statement would be

```
IF DAYS >= 30 AND TOTAL >= 5 THEN CHARGE = LONGDISTANCE + LOCAL
```

In this statement, the AND connective and two logical expressions are used to derive a new compound logical expression. More generally, compound logical expressions involve logical expressions and the use of the AND, OR, and NOT connectives. Consider the following examples:

1. Suppose a programmer wants a statement that would increment a counter N by 1 if and only if two conditions were satisfied, namely, if A is both greater than 90 and less than or equal to 100. Then the following could be used:

   ```
   IF A > 90 AND A < = 100 THEN N = N + 1
   ```

2. If in a program the total sales are to be printed on Friday or when the response to a request for printing the TOTAL is ''yes'' (or if both conditions were true), then the following statement would be appropriate:

   IF DAY$ = ''FRIDAY'' OR RESPONSE$ = ''YES'' THEN PRINT TOTAL

3. If you want to emphasize that a variable X should *not* be negative, then you can use the NOT connective. For example, the next statement says that when X is *not* negative, enter a value for Y into the program.

   IF NOT (X < 0) THEN INPUT Y

   Logically, this statement is equivalent to

   IF X > = 0 THEN INPUT Y

   but in this form the negation of a certain condition is not so clearly emphasized.

The important matter of course is to know when a compound logical expression is true or false so that you can program accordingly. The rules for the AND, OR, and NOT connectives follow, where L1 and L2 represent individual logical expressions.

AND Operator

L1	L2	L1 AND L2
true	true	true
true	false	false
false	true	false
false	false	false

OR Operator

L1	L2	L1 OR L2
true	true	true
true	false	true
false	true	true
false	false	false

NOT Operator

L1	NOT L1
true	false
false	true

How are expressions that contain both the AND and the OR connective evaluated? Suppose A = 1, B = 2 and C = 5. Then is the compound logical expression

A > 2 AND B < 4 OR C = 5

true or false? Does the computer follow the logical development

$$\underbrace{\underbrace{A > 2 \text{ AND } B < 4}_{\text{FALSE}} \text{ OR } \underbrace{C = 5}_{\text{TRUE}}}_{\text{TRUE}}$$

or

$$\underbrace{\underbrace{A > 2}_{\text{FALSE}} \text{ AND } \underbrace{B < 4 \text{ OR } C = 5}_{\text{TRUE}}}_{\text{FALSE}}$$

when determining the value of this logical expression? It is clearly a matter of priorities among the logical operators AND, OR, and NOT (much like the hierarchy of arithmetic operations presented earlier). The following hierarchy is used:

Logical Operator	Priority
NOT	Highest
AND	Intermediate
OR	Lowest

Therefore the above expression involving the AND and OR connectives is true.

The following program uses compound logical expressions with the AND connective.

Program 14.

Step 1. Describe the problem.

A teacher wants to computerize his semester grade report where he has established the percentages of 90, 80, 70, and 60 to earn a grade of A, B, C, and D, respectively. The class is very large, and so the teacher does not wish to determine how many grades are to be given before the program is used. One number is to be entered for each student; the output is the corresponding letter grade.

Step 2. Design the logic of the solution.

A trailer, say -99, and a WHILE/WEND loop will be used because the total number of grades is not known (and thus a limiting value for a FOR/NEXT loop is not available). After checking that a value entered is not the trailer, the appropriate letter grade must be determined. The AND connective in the logical expression of an IF...THEN statement is appropriate. To see why, consider the B grade for grades G in the 80s. The condition can be written G < 90 AND G >= 80. After printing out the letter grade, another grade is entered until finally -99 is encountered to end the program.

Step 3. Code the program.

```
PRINT "ENTER GRADE, AFTER LAST GRADE ENTER -99"
INPUT G
WHILE G < > -99
  IF G >= 90 THEN PRINT "A"
  IF G < 90 AND G >= 80 THEN PRINT "B"
  IF G < 80 AND G >= 70 THEN PRINT "C"
  IF G < 70 AND G >= 60 THEN PRINT "D"
  IF G < 60 THEN PRINT "F"
  INPUT "NEXT GRADE"; G
WEND
END
```

Sample program output:

```
ENTER GRADE, AFTER LAST GRADE ENTER -99
82
B
NEXT GRADE?
91
A
NEXT GRADE?
75
C
NEXT GRADE?
-99
```

Further Notes on Program 14:

1. Only one of the logical expressions to determine the letter grade is true for any value of G.
2. Even if G >= 90 is true, all of the other logical expressions in this program are checked. Therefore this program is not very "elegant". We will reconsider this program when we present multiline IF statements.
3. The flowchart for this program is shown in Figure 2.6.

The IF...THEN...ELSE Statement

Most versions of BASIC, including QB, allow the IF...THEN...ELSE statement. Its general form is

IF logical expression THEN clause ELSE clause

If the logical expression is true, the THEN clause is executed and the ELSE clause is ignored. If the expression is false, the THEN clause is bypassed and the ELSE clause is executed. This situation is depicted in Figure 2.7.

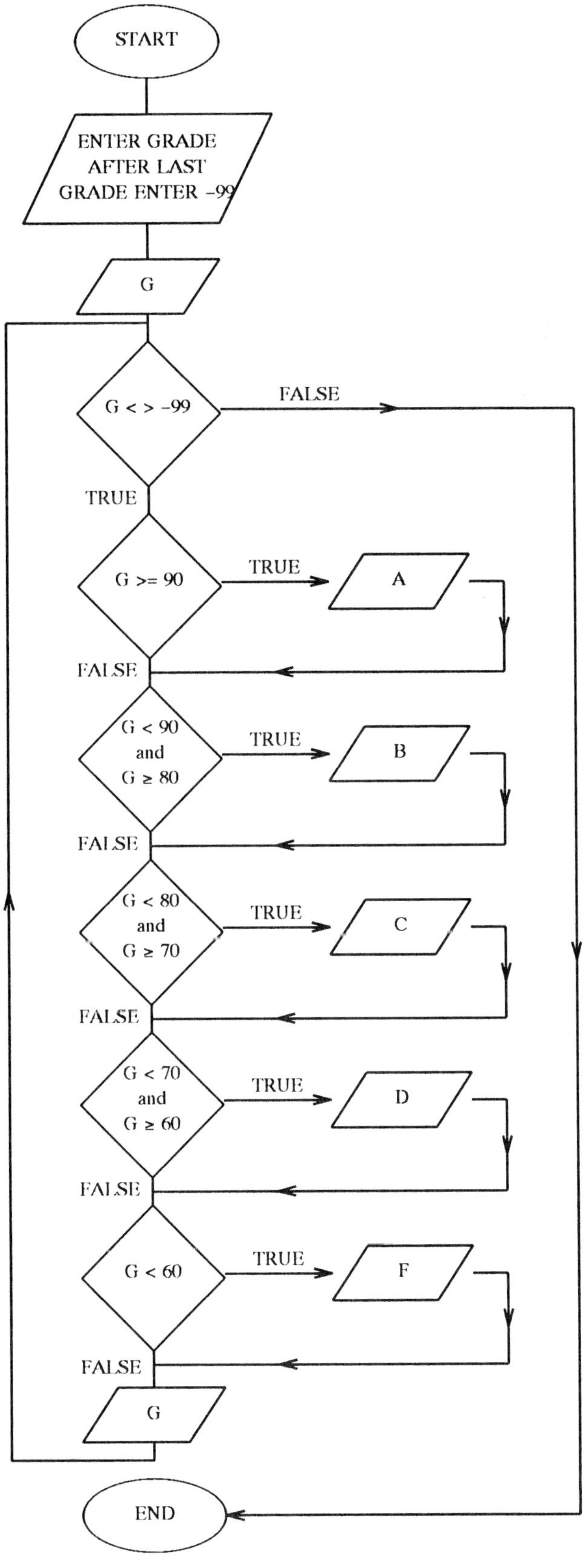

Figure 2.6. Flowchart for Program 14

Consider the following short program to print whether a number entered is positive or not positive:

```
INPUT X
IF X > 0 THEN PRINT "POSITIVE" ELSE PRINT "NOT POSITIVE"
END
```

The reader should note that the same result could be accomplished with two IF...THEN statements instead of one IF...THEN...ELSE statement:

```
INPUT X
IF X > 0 THEN PRINT "POSITIVE"
IF X <= 0 THEN PRINT "NOT POSITIVE"
END
```

The Multiline IF Statement

Many applications require that more than just one action be performed when a logical assertion is either true or false. QuickBASIC's multiline IF statement allows you to write THEN and ELSE blocks containing two or more statements. The general form is

```
IF logical expression THEN
   statement(s)
ELSE
   statement(s)
END IF
```

Note that the first line must terminate with the keyword THEN, and the last line must have a space between the keywords END and IF. The END IF tells QB where the end of your ELSE clause is and therefore must be included. The following program uses the multiline IF statement.

Program 15.

Step 1. Describe the problem.

A teacher needs a computer program to count and print the number of passing and failing grades in each of his classes. A grade of 60 is needed to pass. The input will be a set of grades for a particular class. The output should consist of each grade, a message as to whether that grade results in passing or failing, and finally a summary stating the number of passing and failing grades.

Step 2. Design the logic of the solution.

The first step is to initialize two counters to 0, NPASS for the number of passing grades and NFAIL for the number of failing grades. Because the number of grades will vary from class to class, a teacher should be able to enter the number of students N each time he runs the program. A FOR/NEXT loop can then be used, with a limit value N, to print each grade with the appropriate PASS or FAIL message. A multiline IF statement will be used to decide which message to print and to increment the appropriate counter for passing or failing grades.

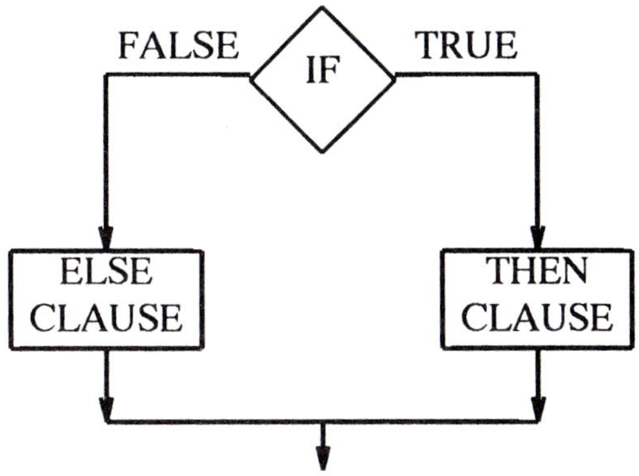

Figure 2.7. IF...THEN...ELSE Statement Flow

Step 3. Code the program.

```
REM  PROGRAM TO COUNT AND PRINT NUMBER OF
REM  PASSING AND FAILING GRADES

REM ********* INITIALIZING SUMMING VARIABLES *******
LET NPASS = 0
LET NFAIL = 0

REM ********* ESTABLISHING THE LOOP ****************
INPUT ''ENTER TOTAL NUMBER OF GRADES''; N
PRINT ''ENTER A GRADE AFTER EACH QUESTION MARK''.

REM ********* PROCESSING THE GRADES ****************
FOR I = 1 TO N
  INPUT GRADE
  IF GRADE < 60 THEN
     PRINT ''FAIL''
     NFAIL = NFAIL + 1
  ELSE
     PRINT ''PASS''
     NPASS = NPASS + 1
  END IF
NEXT I
PRINT

REM ********* PRINTING A SUMMARY *****************
PRINT NPASS; ''PASSING GRADES''
PRINT NFAIL; ''FAILING GRADES''
END
```

Sample Output:

```
ENTER TOTAL NUMBER OF GRADES? 6
ENTER A GRADE AFTER EACH QUESTION MARK.
? 79
PASS
? 58
FAIL
? 93
PASS
? 89
PASS
? 60
PASS
? 57
FAIL

4 PASSING GRADES
2 FAILING GRADES
```

The multiline IF can be extended to include any number of ELSEIF clauses. The general form is

```
IF logical expression THEN
   statement(s)
ELSEIF logical expression THEN
   statement(s)
ELSEIF logical expression THEN
   statement(s)
   .
   .
   .
ELSE
   statement(s)
END IF
```

Note that there is no space in the single keyword ELSEIF and only one ELSE clause can appear. The clauses evaluate sequentially and as soon as one clause is true, the associated set of statement(s) is executed. Control then passes to the next executable statement after the END IF. If all of the ELSEIF clauses are false (or there are no ELSEIF clauses, as was the case in Program 15), then the statements associated with the ELSE clause are executed.

Let's now rewrite Program 14 to incorporate the multiline IF statement. You may recall that in that grading program, all of the logical expressions were checked on each execution of the program (except when G = -99). This redundant checking of logical expressions can be eliminated by the multiline IF as shown below.

Program 16.

```
REM GRADING PROGRAM USING THE MORE EFFICIENT MULTILINE IF
PRINT "ENTER GRADE, AFTER LAST GRADE ENTER -99"
INPUT G
WHILE G < > -99
  IF G >= 90 THEN
     PRINT "A"
  ELSEIF G >= 80 THEN
     PRINT "B"
  ELSEIF G >= 70 THEN
     PRINT "C"
  ELSEIF G >= 60 THEN
     PRINT "D"
  ELSE
     PRINT "F"
  END IF
  INPUT "NEXT GRADE"; G
WEND
END
```

Further Notes on Program 16:

1. Note how the compound expressions with the AND connective in Program 14 can now be reduced to simple expressions.
2. The ordering of the clauses is very important here. Why?

The SELECT CASE Statement

The SELECT CASE statement can be thought of as a multi-way branch (i.e., a means by which a program can select one of a multiple number of selection alternatives). The appropriate branch is based upon the value of an expression. Its general form is

```
SELECT CASE expression
CASE constant list
  statement(s)
CASE constant list
  statement(s)
   .
   .
   .
CASE ELSE
  statement(s)
END SELECT
```

If the value of the expression matches the value in a CASE constant list, that CASE block of statements is executed. You can use as many CASE blocks as you have options to perform. The SELECT CASE also offers a CASE ELSE block that can be executed if the value of the expression matches none of the values in the constant lists. The ELSE clause can be omitted. After execution of the appropriate block of statements, control is passed to the statement following END SELECT.

As an example, consider the following:

```
SELECT CASE GRADE$
CASE "A"
   NUMA = NUMA + 1
CASE "B"
   NUMB = NUMB + 1
CASE "C"
   NUMC = NUMC + 1
CASE "D"
   NUMD = NUMD + 1
CASE "F"
   NUMF = NUMF + 1
CASE ELSE
   PRINT "INCORRECT LETTER GRADE"; GRADE$
END SELECT
```

This structure uses the value of the variable GRADE$ to determine which CASE statement block to execute. For example, if the value of GRADE$ is "A" then the statement NUMA = NUMA + 1 is executed. Similarly, if the value of GRADE$ matches any of the other constants, then that corresponding counter is incremented by 1. If GRADE$ matches none of the constants listed, then the CASE ELSE block is executed.

Many times the determination of which CASE statement block to execute does not depend on a single constant, but rather on a range of constants. For example, let us reconsider Program 14, our letter grade determination program. You know that to receive an "A" the grade G had to be 90 or above. Thus you could write

```
SELECT CASE G
CASE 90, 91, 92, 93, 94, 95, 96, 97, 98, 99, 100
   PRINT "A"
```

However, the SELECT CASE statement allows the use of ranges in the following forms:

CASE constant TO constant

CASE IS relational operator constant

Thus the above example could be written using the constant-to-constant form as

```
SELECT CASE G
CASE 90 TO 100
   PRINT "A"
```

or using the >= relational operator form as

```
SELECT CASE G
CASE IS >= 90
   PRINT "A"
```

It is left to you as an exercise to rewrite Program 14 using the SELECT CASE statement. As was the case with the multiline IF approach, the use of SELECT CASE would make Program 14 run more efficiently, since you'll avoid checking a sequence of IF statements on each execution of the program.

In the next program, the user is given a set of options in a menu, from which he or she is to choose one item. The SELECT CASE statement is used in this program to handle the branching based on the user's choice from the menu.

Program 17.

Step 1. Describe the problem.

Write a program to either add, subtract, multiply, or divide two numbers entered at a terminal. The user must be able to choose which mathematical operation is to be performed. Allow the user to enter more than one pair of numbers. Output the answer after each operation is executed.

Step 2. Design the logic of the solution.

After two numbers are entered from the terminal, the program should display a menu with a selection for each of the four mathematical operations and a selection to end the program. To implement an SELECT CASE statement, the user can select the numbers 1, 2, 3, 4, or 5 as his choice from the menu. The SELECT CASE statement will then allow the appropriate branching.

Step 3. Code the program.

```
REM  ARITHMETIC OPERATIONS WITH SELECT CASE
PRINT

REM  ******* SELECTING FROM A MENU **********
PRINT "CHOOSE ONE OF THE FOLLOWING:"
PRINT
PRINT "1. ADDITION"
PRINT "2. SUBTRACTION"
PRINT "3. MULTIPLICATION"
PRINT "4. DIVISION"
PRINT "5. END THE PROGRAM"
PRINT
INPUT "ENTER 1, 2, 3, 4, OR 5:";CHOICE
IF CHOICE < > 5 THEN INPUT "ENTER TWO NUMBERS"; X, Y

REM ******** PROCESSING THE CHOICE **********
WHILE CHOICE < > 5
```

```
  SELECT CASE CHOICE
   CASE 1
     PRINT X;"+";Y;"=";X + Y
   CASE 2
     PRINT X;"-";Y;"=";X - Y
   CASE 3
     PRINT X;"*";Y;"=";X*Y
   CASE 4
     PRINT X;"/";Y;"=";X / Y
   CASE ELSE
     REM THIS BLOCK HELPS TO PREVENT ERROR MESSAGES
  END SELECT
INPUT "ENTER 1, 2, 3, 4, OR 5:";CHOICE
WEND
PRINT "HOPE YOU HAD FUN!"
END
```

Sample output:

```
CHOOSE ONE OF THE FOLLOWING:

1. ADDITION
2. SUBTRACTION
3. MULTIPLICATION
4. DIVISION
5. END THE PROGRAM

ENTER 1, 2, 3, 4, OR 5:? 2

ENTER TWO NUMBERS? 5, 4

5 - 4 = 1

ENTER 1, 2, 3, 4, OR 5:? 3

5 * 4 = 20

ENTER 1, 2, 3, 4, OR 5:? 5

HOPE YOU HAD FUN!
```

Further Notes on Program 17:

1. The CASE ELSE is used to avoid error messages resulting from values out of the range of the SELECT CASE values. Wrong values will be ignored and the user will be prompted for another choice.
2. This program is designed so that a user has the option of performing two operations on the same pair of numbers by simply entering another choice.
3. Note that the menu is printed only once for each execution. For another application, it might be helpful to reprint the menu each time a new selection is made. We will consider an elegant way to do this using subroutines in Chapter Three.

4. Executing the statement in the CASE 4 block could result in an attempt to divide by zero, which would lead to an error message. You are invited to modify this program so that a check is made to be sure that a divisor is not zero.
5. The flowchart for this program is shown in Figure 2.8.

F. STRUCTURED PROGRAMMING AND THE GOTO STATEMENT

Up to this point in the text, you have not seen the use of a single GOTO statement, even though the GOTO is available in QB. The GOTO statement accomplishes an unconditional branch (i.e., the flow of execution is altered by the GOTO statement each time this statement is encountered). The next statement to be executed is the one whose line number or label is specified in the GOTO statement. Programmers who are not careful with GOTOs can end up with code containing all sorts of transfers, which makes the code extremely difficult to understand and modify. A goal in software development is to produce programs that are easy to understand and modify, where the logic flow of the program is easily followed. Branching to a line that is not the next one sequentially in a program does not lend itself to good program structure.

In terms of the understandability of a program, the GOTO is often ambiguous because it can be used for a variety of tasks in a program. For example, you can use a GOTO to branch around a piece of code that is meant to be executed under a different set of conditions, or to form a repetition structure, or to branch to a shared piece of code. A language, such as QuickBASIC, lends itself to understandability if it has unique language statements to accomplish each of these tasks. (See Table 2.1.) Note that the QB constructs listed in Table 2.1 more clearly define their objective than the more general GOTO.

GOTO Task	QB Construct
branch around code	IF THEN ELSE blocks Multiline IF SELECT CASE
perform repetition	FOR/NEXT WHILE/WEND
branch to shared code	subroutines functions procedures

Table 2.1

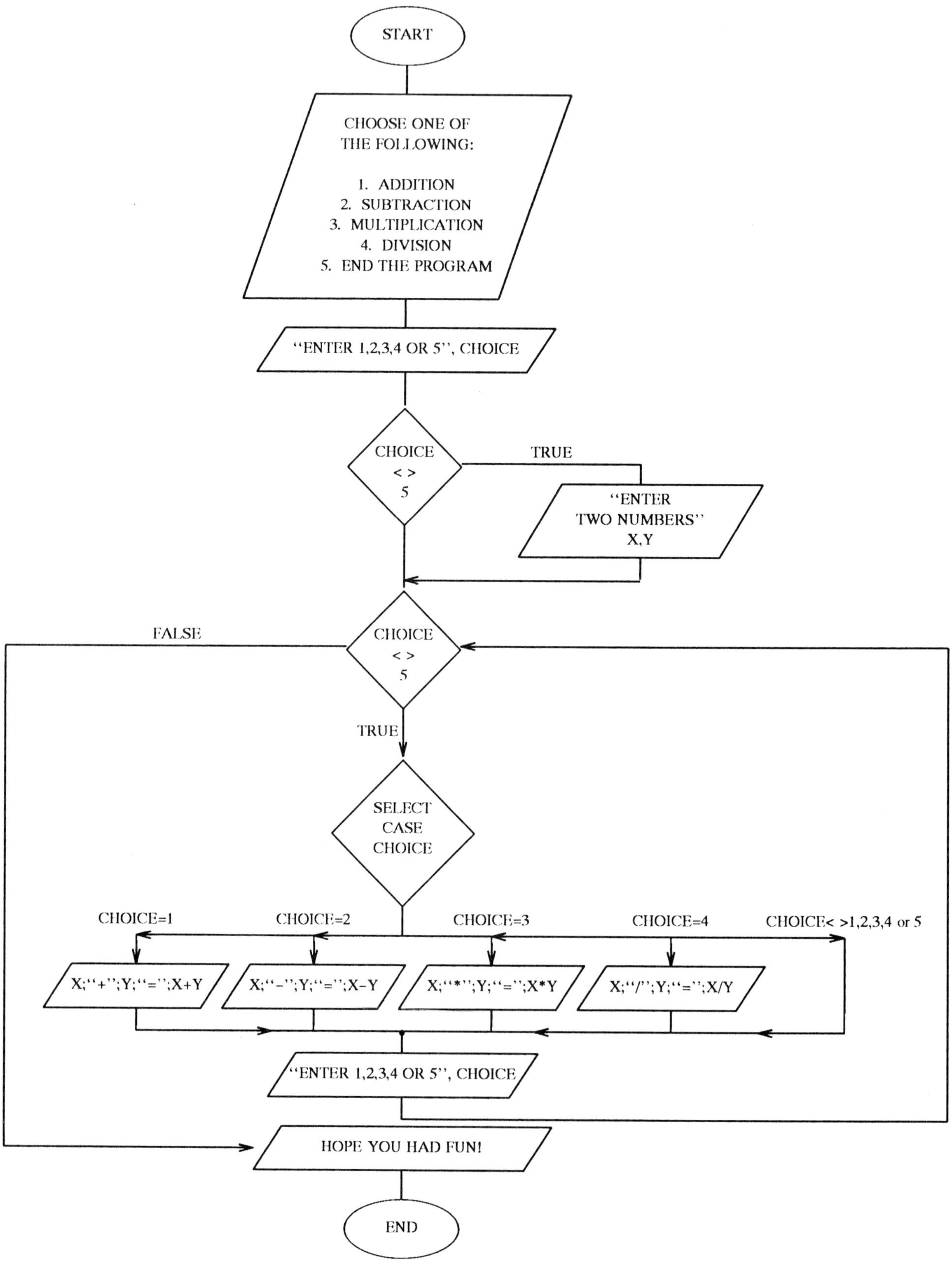

Figure 2.8. Arithmetic operations with a select case.

Avoiding the GOTO statement is only one step toward structured programming. Your task as a programmer will be to develop programs that are easy to understand and modify, and this is most easily achieved by using sequence, selection, and repetition structures, as seen in this chapter, which have one entry point and one exit point. (See Figure 2.3.) Using a structured programming approach allows you to think of the entire program as a sequence of blocks of code, each performing a specific task. This "divide and conquer" approach is essential when developing large software programs.

Consider the block diagram of a program shown in Figure 2.9a. Note how each of the parts is constructed from a control structure. Note also how you can view the program from a global perspective (an overview of the whole), seeing the five blocks as part of a whole program, or from inner levels of detail, where you may be interested in the logic of a single block. The structure of the program lends itself to understandability at various levels. In Figure 2.9b, the use of a single GOTO distorts your view of the program as a set of blocks. You can no longer view the IF...THEN...ELSE block at an inner level of detail without at once being forced to comprehend the global level of the entire program. Furthermore, the labeled statements in Figure 2.9b cannot be considered a block (note that the rectangle around these statements in Figure 2.9a has been removed in Figure 2.9b) because these statements are directly tied to the GOTO. You cannot simply remove these statements without reflecting a change in the IF...THEN...ELSE structure. This entangling of various levels of detail makes this program intrinsically harder to understand.

In the next chapter, you will study several QuickBASIC constructs that can help you develop well-structured programs.

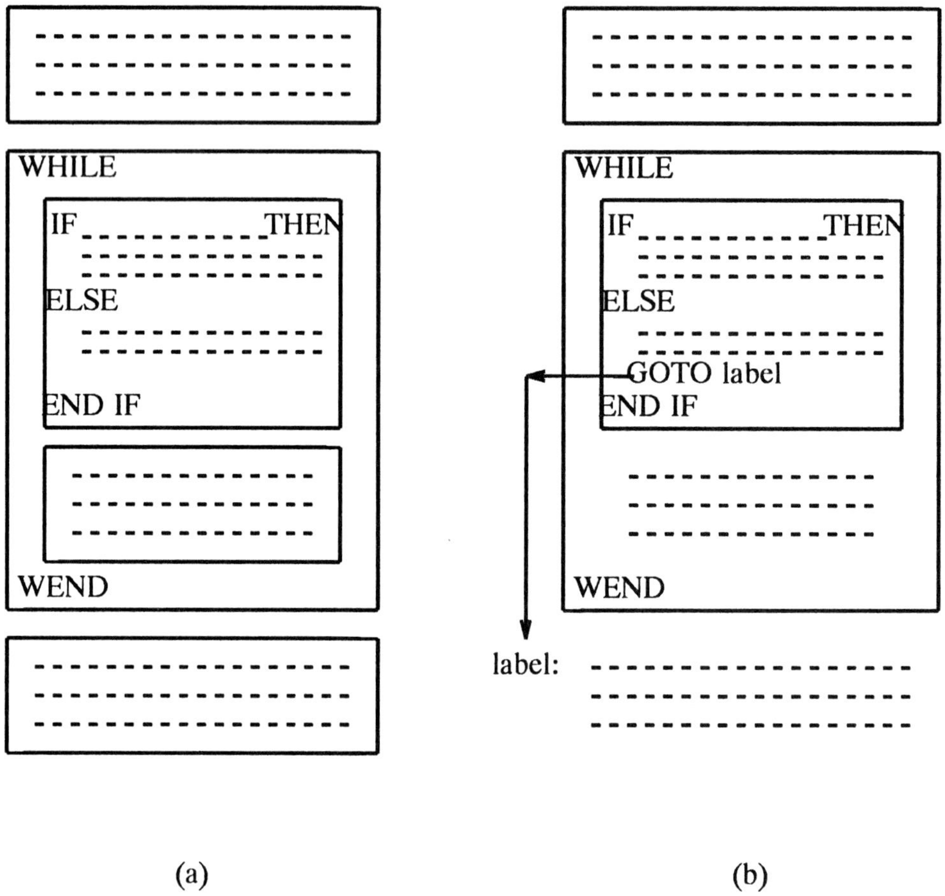

Figure 2.9. (a) Structured Program; (b) Unstructured Program

G. REVIEW EXERCISES

1. Draw a flowchart for Program 4.
2. Rewrite Program 3 using a WHILE/WEND pair of statements.
3. Using a FOR/NEXT loop, rewrite Program 2 to handle 10 employees on a single run. The output should be the employee number (1-40), rate, hours and pay. Supply your own rate and hours for each employee.
4. Use a FOR/NEXT loop to accomplish each of the following tasks:
   (a) Print the numbers 5, 4, 3, 2, 1, 0 in this order.
   (b) Print the numbers -6, -3, 0, 3, 6 in this order.

5. What is the value of SUM after these program segments?

(a)

```
SUM = 0
FOR I = 1 TO 5
FOR J = 1 TO 3
LET SUM = SUM + J
NEXT J
NEXT I
```

(b)

```
SUM  = 0
FOR I = 1 TO 5
FOR J = 1 TO 3
SUM = SUM + I + J
NEXT J
NEXT I
```

6. Indicate the EXACT output produced by each of the following QuickBASIC programs.

(a)

```
LET A = 10
LET B = 5
IF A < 5 OR B > 10 THEN PRINT A + B
LET C = A + B
IF B > A THEN PRINT A ELSE PRINT C
END
```

(b)

```
SUM = 1
WHILE SUM < 100
  SUM = SUM * 2
  PRINT SUM
WEND
END
```

(c)

```
FOR I = 2 TO 3
  FOR J = 1 TO 4
     PRINT J
  NEXT J
NEXT I
END
```

(d)

```
LET T = 7
WHILE T > 0
READ A
PRINT A
IF A = 4 THEN RESTORE
LET T = T - 2
WEND
DATA 8, 5, 4, 9, 6, 5, 1
END
```

7. What are the values (T or F) of the following logical assertions, given that A = 2, B = 9, and C = 5?

   (a) A = 2

   (b) A < B AND C >= A

   (c) B > A AND NOT C < A OR C = 5

8. Referring to Program 7, what problem arises if -1 is the first number entered into the program? Modify Program 7 (include an IF...THEN statement to check the value of COUNT) so that this problem is avoided.

9. Rewrite Program 14 using a SELECT CASE statement.

H. LAB EXERCISES

1. Enter the following program into your computer:

```
FOR I = 1 TO 100
   PRINT I,
NEXT I
END
```

Execute the program by pulling down the Run menu and selecting "Start".

What happens? Be precise.

____

____

After the statement "NEXT I" add another statement PRINT I.

Execute the program again.

What value is printed for this statement? __________

Suppose you want to print the numbers 2,4,6,8,...100. Make the appropriate changes to the program to produce this printout. Execute the program.

Write the program here.

____

____

____

____

____

____

Next, suppose you would like to have a program that prints the numbers 1 to any number that you desire. For example, you would like to have the numbers from 1 to 29 printed out. The next time, you might want the numbers from 1 to 36 printed out. This requires that the limit on the FOR loop be a variable. "It varies!!" Thus give it the variable name LIMIT. Now, how can you assign a value to LIMIT with each execution? You have already done this and the QuickBASIC statement that does this is ________________. Enter the "improved" program here. Don't forget to add a prompt telling the user what to enter. Execute the program to make sure it works.

____

____

____

____

____

____

____

Now, you want more control over the series of numbers that need to printed out. You no longer want to always start at 1. What parameter of the FOR loop must you change?

____

Call the new variable INIT. Make the appropriate changes. Execute this program. What happens if INIT > LIMIT? Try it.

____

____

Write the new program below.

____

____

____

____

____

____

____

____

2. You have talked about nested loops. What does it mean to be nested?

____

You now want to write a program that prints the numbers from 1 through 5 ten times. You can accomplish this without nested loops with the following program:

```
FOR J = 1 TO 10
  PRINT "1  2  3  4  5"
NEXT J
```

First try writing this program with nested loops. Notice that you need to do the printing of the numbers 1 through 5 ten times. The loop that controls the number of times the set of numbers is printed will become the outer loop. Notice that for each time through the outer loop, you want to print 1 2 3 4 5. The loop that controls which number is to be printed will become the inner loop.

Enter the following statements:

```
FOR J = 1 TO 10
   FOR K = 1 to 5
      PRINT K;
   NEXT K
   PRINT
NEXT J
```

Run the program. What is the output?

____
____
____
____
____
____
____
____
____
____

What do you think the statement PRINT does? Try running the program without it. Write the results below.

____
____
____
____
____

What constant(s) would you change to print 1 through 5 twenty times? ____________

What constant(s) would you change to print the numbers 10 through 20 ten times?
____

3. Type in the following program.

```
PRINT "WHICH WOULD YOU LIKE A (C)ARROT OR A (P)EACH?"
INPUT ANSWER$
IF ANSWER$ = "C" THEN PRINT "YOU CHOSE A VEGETABLE"
IF ANSWER$ = "P" THEN PRINT "YOU CHOSE A FRUIT"
END
```

What happens when you type "C" as input?

What happens when you type "c" as input?

Rewrite the third statement to prevent this from happening.

What happens when you type "P" as input?

What happens when you type "p" as input?

Rewrite the fourth statement to prevent this from happening.

What happens when you type "K" as input? WHY?

Write a statement that checks whether the input was one of the available selections and another that gives a message saying that the choice was not one of the possibilities.

Where should these statements appear?

Notice how important it is to test your program with many possible inputs and to make allowances (code) for those that don't make sense.

Now add another selection for another fruit, the banana. Rewrite the program for the addition of the banana selection, using a multiline IF statement.

4. Enter and run the following:

```
PRINT "HOW OLD ARE YOU?"
INPUT A
IF A = 18 THEN PRINT "YOU ARE OLD ENOUGH TO VOTE"
IF A > 18 THEN PRINT "YOU ARE OLD ENOUGH TO VOTE"
IF A < 18 THEN PRINT "YOU ARE NOT OLD ENOUGH TO VOTE"
END
```

The third and fourth statements could easily be combined by changing the relational expression. What would the new line look like?

____

Rewrite this program so that it uses an IF...THEN...ELSE construction.

____

____

____

____

____

____

____

5. Type in the following program:

```
INPUT C
PRINT "BEFORE THE WHILE LOOP"
WHILE C < 10
  PRINT C;
  C = C + 1
WEND
PRINT "AFTER THE WHILE LOOP"
```

Show the output produced by the program when the variable C is initialized to each of the following values. Also explain why this happens.

C = 1

____

____

C = 10

____

____

C = -5

____

____

C = 100

6. Input the following program and run it with these values: A = 10, B = 20, and C = 30

```
REM ANOTHER LOOK AT THE INPUT STATEMENT
INPUT "ENTER THREE NUMBERS"; A, B, C
D = A + B + C
E = A * B * C
F = C - B - A
PRINT "A + B + C = "; D
PRINT "A * B * C = "; E
PRINT "C - B - A = "; F
END
```

What is the output of this program?

Rewrite the above program using READ/DATA statements. Run it with the same values. Write the new program below.

What is the output?

How does the READ instruction differ from the INPUT instruction?

7. Many times the first value in a DATA statement has an important meaning (for example, the number of times a loop is executed). Enter the following program below and run it.

```
TOTAL = 0
READ LIMIT
FOR K = 1 TO LIMIT
   READ A
   TOTAL = TOTAL + A
NEXT K
PRINT "THE SUM IS "; TOTAL
DATA 7,12,45,24,55,77,88,99
END
```

What is the value of LIMIT? ________

Give the values for the variables listed below on each execution of the FOR loop.

LIMIT	K	A	TOTAL

What is the final value of TOTAL? ________

Could you have used the following set of DATA statements in the above program and still receive the same answer?

```
DATA 7
DATA 12
DATA 45
DATA 24,55,77
DATA 88,99
```

____

What is it that really matters concerning DATA statements?

____

____

If you want to add the numbers 23,54,77,23,77,88,90,22,44,66,37,88, write the DATA statement for the above program that would do the job.

____

8. Many times the last value of a DATA statement or the very last value of all the DATA statements has an important meaning. Enter the code below and execute it.

```
TOTAL = 0
READ A
WHILE A <> -9999
   TOTAL = TOTAL + A
   READ A
WEND
PRINT "THE TOTAL IS "; TOTAL
DATA 55,55,77,88,99,-9999
END
```

Give the values for the variables listed below on each execution of the WHILE loop.

A	Total	A (again after READ A)

What is the final value of total? ________

When does the condition on the WHILE loop become false?

____

Replace the current DATA statement with DATA -9999. Run the program. What is the output? Explain why.

____

____

Replace the current DATA statement with DATA 60,50,40,0. Run the program again. What is the output and why?

____

____

How many values can be summed up using this program?

____

What happens if -9999 is part of the series that you need to sum? What should you do?

____

____

____

Do you see why -9999 is called a trailer?

How many DATA statements can I have for this program?

____

9. Consider the following program that processes restaurant orders:

```
REM  DUMPY'S BURGERS RESTAURANT HAS ASSIGNED A
REM  CODE NUMBER FOR EACH ITEM ON ITS MENU
REM          CODE#          ITEM
REM            1            SHAKE
REM            2            SOFT DRINK
REM            3            FRIES
REM            4            HAMBURGER
REM            5            JUMBO BURGER
REM            6            END OF ORDER

REM ************ ENTER ORDER ******************
TOTAL = 0
INPUT "ENTER CODE NUMBER";C
WHILE C < > 6
  INPUT "ENTER QUANTITY";Q

REM ************ PROCESS ORDER ****************
  SELECT CASE C
    CASE 1
      COST = .60 * Q
      PRINT Q; "SHAKES", "$"; COST
    CASE 2
      COST = .40 * Q
      PRINT Q; "SOFT DRINKS", "$"; COST
    CASE 3
      COST = .50 * Q
      PRINT Q; "FRIES", "$"; COST
    CASE 4
      COST = 1.00 * Q
      PRINT Q; "HAMBURGERS", "$"; COST
    CASE 5
      COST = 1.50 * Q
      PRINT Q; "JUMBO BURGERS", "$"; COST
    CASE ELSE
  END SELECT

REM ************ FINDING THE TOTAL ************
  TOTAL = TOTAL + COST
  INPUT "ENTER CODE NUMBER"; C
WEND

REM ************ TOTAL ORDER ******************
```

```
PRINT "TOTAL ORDER IS"; TOTAL
END
```

Enter the following orders into the program:

2 HAMBURGER, 3 SOFT DRINKS, AND 2 FRIES
3 HAMBURGER, 1 SHAKE
4 HAMBURGERS
2 JUMBO BURGERS, 2 SHAKES

(a) What is printed when the program is run for each order?

____

(b) How are various quantities of each item handled in the program?

____

(c) What in the program checks for the end of an order?

____

10. Fill in the blanks in the following code to construct a complete program that would produce the output shown below. Try your program.

```
10   FOR I = ________________
20     ________________
30       PRINT ________________
40     NEXT J
50   ________________
60   END
```

Output:

```
1 + 1 = 2
1 + 2 = 3
1 + 3 = 4
2 + 1 = 3
2 + 2 = 4
2 + 3 = 5
```

I. PROGRAMMING PROBLEMS

1. A company agrees to pay one of its employees $1 on the first day of work and to double the wage for every day worked thereafter. Thus the employee receives $1 the first day, $2 the second day, $4 the third day, and so on. The employee works for the company for 30 days. Write a program using a FOR/NEXT loop to determine the amount of money paid to the employee each day worked. Also accumulate the total of the earnings. There is no input for this program. Your program should produce the following table as output.

PAY SCHEDULE FOR 30 DAYS
(Skip two lines)

DAY #	DAY'S PAY	TOTAL PAY
	(Skip one line)	
1	1	1
2	2	3
3	4	7
4	8	15
.	.	.
.	.	.
.	.	.
30		

Organize the format of your program so that the title of the table is approximately centered on the page and so that column headings are printed in the first, third, and fifth print fields, respectively.

2. Listed below by identification number are the employees who work for the company Computers International. Also listed are the number of years with the company and the annual salary for each employee. A computer program is needed to find the
   (a) average salary of all employees who have been employed 10 or more years,
   (b) average salary of all employees who have been employed less than 10 years,
   (c) average number of years employed and the average salary for all of the employees listed.

   Input data will include each employee's identification number, years employed, and annual salary. The program should use a FOR/NEXT loop to process exactly ten sets of input data.

   Output should be in tabular form, listing all input data and all required averages. Supply headings and other descriptive information to identify the output. Put the following data in DATA statements and use these to test the program:

Identification Number	Years Employed	Annual Salary
1425	7	31000
1603	2	18000
1555	11	37000
1439	14	43500
1611	18	55400
1911	1	17500
2001	8	40000
1777	2	25000
1356	4	27500
1600	5	29000

3. Extend the program you wrote for Programming Problem 2 to accomplish the following tasks:

   (a) After an appropriate heading, list the employees by identification number who have been employed more than ten years or are making at least $40,000.

   (b) Then, after another heading, list those employees by identification number who have been employed less than three years and are making over $25,000.

4. Your office purchases five different products whose retail prices are shown in the following table:

Product Number	Unit Price
1	$3.75
2	5.25
3	2.50
4	14.60
5	8.35

   Each month a purchase report indicating the number of items purchased of each type and total dollars spent must be completed. You are to computerize this function. Use the following guidelines:

   (a) Use a FOR/NEXT structure to control the loop.

   (b) Use READ/DATA instructions to input the data.

   (c) Use a SELECT CASE statement to help determine the retail price for each product.

   (d) Calculate the amount spent for a given number of items and print a table similar to the following. Output the total expenditure below the table.

Product #	Quantity	Price	Amount
2	20	$5.00	$100.00

(e) Test your program, using the following 12 pairs of data.

Prod. #	Qty	Prod. #	Qty.	Prod. #	Qty.
3	22	5	2	3	1
5	24	4	7	4	1
2	5	3	2	1	10
1	1	2	30	2	14

5. Modify the program you wrote for Problem 4 to include a discount for bulk purchases. In other words, if enough items of a given product are ordered, the wholesaler sells them at a cheaper price per unit item. Using the following additional price structure, repeat steps (d) and (e) above.

Product Number	Bulk Unit Price
1	For 5 or more, $3.50
2	For 3 or more, $5.00
3	For 7 or more, $2.20
4	For 2 or more, $14.00
5	For 4 or more, $8.00

6. With vacation time coming up, you and your friends decide that it is time to get away. Although your first thought was to vacation in Florida, all agreed that vacation in the sunshine state was just too commonplace. So, after extensive research by your travel agent, you discover a little hideaway in the Bahamas called *Bob's Bahamian Bunkhouse*. While all were ecstatic at the idea of a tropical siesta, they also worried about over-extending their tight student budgets.

"Don't worry about the cost," Bob assured them. "I'll give you a special bunkhouse rate: one dollar the first day, and each day after that is just twice your bill through the day before." Well, this made your group so excited they decided to stay an extra week. Your job is to write a BASIC program to calculate your daily bunkhouse rent and total, as well as your final 14-day bunkhouse bill. Hint: the total amount of money M that would be owed on a given day would be calculated by

$$M = Y * 2 + Y$$

where Y is the total amount owed the day before.

Your program should print the headings shown below and should use FOR/NEXT statements to print a 14-line table showing the results. Organize the format of your output so that the title of the table is centered on the page (of 72 spaces) and so that column headings are printed in the first, third, and fifth print fields, respectively. Finally, print a total line telling how much Bob will earn from his little Bahamian bonanza. Your table should look like:

BOB'S BAHAMIAN BUNKHOUSE
Two-Week Billing Report

(Skip two lines)

Day #	Daily Charge	Current Total
1	1	1
2	2	3
3	6	9
.	.	.
.	.	.
.	.	.
14	.	.

Total bill for the group is $ _______________

7. Well, your vacation is over now (assuming you did Programming Problem 6 above; if not, go back and read it quickly) and your group is back early from their stay at Bob's Bahamian Bunkhouse. While the first few days were nice, the room rent started getting pretty steep, and moreover, an unexpected tropical storm forced your group homeward prematurely. Bob felt so terrible about the vacation-ruining storm that he offered a discount to any one of his popular resorts on numerous islands – all reportedly hurricane-free. Given Bob's track record, however, your group wised up and decided to check on these "tropical paradises". Naturally, the display of this research is the heart of this problem!

   Help run a check on Bob by writing a BASIC program that incorporates READ, DATA, RESTORE, and selection statements. (Choose any selection structure you wish.) Your program should use the DATA statements below to supply the information concerning Bob's resort islands, along with their annual hurricane frequencies. It should scan the data initially to calculate and print out an average of all frequencies. Then it should print out two lists: one for islands whose hurricane frequencies are below the average, and another for those whose frequencies are at least as big as the average. Because your friends have been to the Bahamian resort, it should show up in the second list, regardless of its hurricane frequency. The lists should include the island name in the second print column and the number of hurricanes in the third. (Hint: your program will READ through the entire set of data more than once; hence the need for the RESTORE statement.) Use these data statements in your program:

```
DATA Virgin, 6, San Isabel, 4, Bahamian, 3, Tobago, 8, Maui, 2, Tahiti
DATA 12, Cayman, 10, Trinidad, 9, South Padre, 1, Gilligan's, 5
```

   Your output should include appropriate headings to look something like this:

Average annual number of Bob's islands' hurricanes is ???

Good Vacation Spots

Island	# Hurricanes
xxxxxxxx	xx
yyyyyy	yy

Places to Avoid

Island	# Hurricanes
aaaaaaaa	aa
bbbbbb	bb

CHAPTER THREE

FUNCTIONS AND SUBROUTINES

"Some programs are elegant, some are exquisite, some are sparkling. My claim is that it is possible to write grand programs, noble programs, truly magnificent ones!" (Donald Knuth, 1974, Turing Award Lecture, *Communications of the ACM (17, 12)*, December 1974.)

A. INTRODUCTION

Functions and subroutines provide tremendous power and versatility when programming in QuickBASIC. They are essential tools that you can use to design sophisticated yet logically simple application programs.

Functions in QuickBASIC are true functions in a mathematical sense. Some functions are built into the QB system and are available for use by simply mentioning them by name in a QB program. These are called *built-in (or intrinsic) functions*. You can also define your own function for a particular application. When such functions are formally defined in a program, they are known as *user-defined functions*.

It may happen that a program needs to execute a sequence of code at various times in a program. Instead of duplicating the same program segment in different parts of the program, you can write the segment once as a subroutine. The subroutine can then be referenced from more than one point in the program. This approach often improves the appearance and understandability of the program.

Up to now, all of the programs in this text have consisted of a single unit called the *main program*. With the addition of functions and subroutines, a program can be designed as a collection of units or modules. This approach will facilitate the use of structured programming and the understandability of QuickBASIC programs.

In this chapter, built-in functions, single-line user-defined functions, function procedures, and subroutines are presented.

B. BUILT-IN FUNCTIONS

Almost all versions of BASIC have a number of built-in functions that are used frequently in programming. Some of these functions operate on numerical operands, while others operate on string operands. Mathematical functions are presented in this chapter, and character string functions are covered in Chapter Five.

In general, a built-in function frees the programmer from actually having to develop the lines of code to obtain a particular result. For example, if you need the value of the square root of 37, you do not need to code a FOR/NEXT loop to employ a standard algebraic technique of dividing and averaging over and over until a desired approximation to the square root of 37 is achieved. You only need to use the built-in function, SQR(X) in one line of code such as

```
LET S = SQR(37)
```

The most common mathematical built-in functions are listed in Tables 3.1a, 3.1b, and 3.1c. The operand X in these functions can be any legal QB arithmetic expression.

Function	Meaning
SQR(X)	square root of X
ABS(X)	absolute value of X (if X ≥ 0, then ABS(X) = X; if X < 0, then ABS(X) = -X)
SGN(X)	algebraic sign of X (if X > 0, then SGN(X) = 1; if X = 0, then SGN(X) = 0; if X < 0, then SGN(X) = -1)
INT(X)	greatest integer less than or equal to X
FIX(X)	strips off the fractional part of X
CINT(X)	returns the closest integer to X
RND	produces a random number between 0 and 1

Table 3.1a. Some Common Built-in Functions

The next set of functions listed are the logarithmic and exponential functions. Although you may not use these functions in a QB program very often, they are included here for completeness.

Function	Meaning
EXP(X)	exponential function e^x
LOG(X)	natural logarithm of X (base e)

Table 3.1b. Built-in Exponential and Logarithmic Functions

If you need to do some trigonometry in a QB program, the following built-in functions will be useful.

Function	Meaning
SIN(X)	trigonometric sine of X
COS(X)	trigonometric cosine of X
TAN(X)	trigonometric tangent of X
ATN(X)	the angle whose tangent is X

Table 3.1c. Built-in Trigonometric Functions

The argument X in each of the functions in Table 3.1c is measured in radians. You may recall that an angle that measures 180 degrees also measures π radians. More generally, an angle with measure x degrees measures r radians, where

$$r = \pi * x/180$$

Programs using some of the functions in Table 3.1a follow.

Program 18.

Step 1. Describe the problem.

You want to build a table showing numbers and their square roots. For demonstration purposes, let the numbers range from 1 to 25. The output should be a two-column table, with headings.

Step 2. Design the logic of the solution.

A FOR/NEXT loop, with initial value 1 and limit value 25 will serve your purpose nicely. You can print headings before the FOR statement and then use the SQR function within the loop.

Step 3. Code the program.

```
REM  PROGRAM THAT PRINTS TABLE OF SQUARE ROOTS
PRINT "NUMBER", "SQUARE ROOT"
FOR N = 1 TO 25
  PRINT N, SQR(N)
NEXT N
END
```

Output:

```
1          1
2          1.414214
3          1.732051
4          2
5          2.236068
.
.
.
24         4.89898
25         5
```

Further Notes on Program 18:

1. Because the index variable N in the FOR statement is assigned the values 1 to 25, N is also used as the operand for the SQR function where the square roots of these same 25 numbers are desired.
2. The number of decimal places that appear as the result of the SQR function will vary with different versions of BASIC.

The INT(X) Function

The function INT(X) takes a value of X as input and returns the greatest integer less than or equal to X as output. Consider the following examples:

X	INT(X)
4.2	4
7.9	7
12	12
.1	0
-3.4	-4

The last example shows that this function does not simply truncate the fractional part of a number (although for non-negative values, the result is the same as that for truncation). Using a number line model, we can say that for non-integer X, INT(X) returns the value of the first integer to the *left* of X on the number line. Shown in Figure 3.1 are X and INT(X) when X is equal to 1.5 and -1.5.

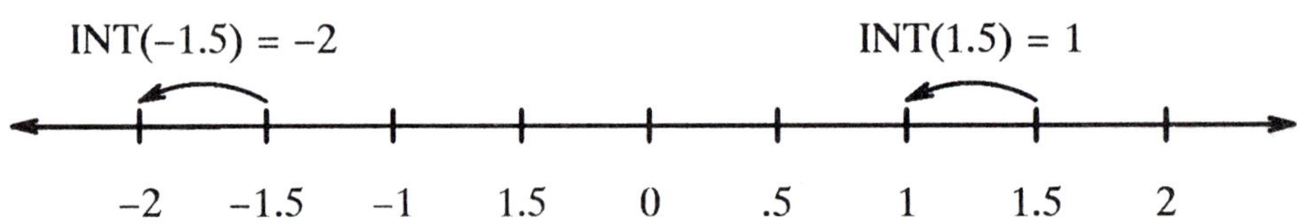

Figure 3.1. Examples of INT(X)

The next program uses INT(X), FIX(X), and CINT(X).

Program 19.

```
REM  PROGRAM THAT READS NUMBERS AND PRINTS
REM  THE GREATEST INTEGER IN EACH NUMBER,
REM  THE NUMBER AFTER TRUNCATING THE FRACTIONAL PART,
REM  AND THE CLOSEST INTEGER TO THE NUMBER.
PRINT "N","INT(N)","FIX(N)","CINT(N)"
READ LIMIT
FOR I = 1 TO LIMIT
  READ N
  PRINT N, INT(N), FIX(N), CINT(N)
```

```
NEXT I
DATA 5, 3.6, 21.441, 0, -3.8, -7.1
END
```

Output:

N	INT(N)	FIX(N)	CINT(N)
3.6	3	3	4
21.441	21	21	21
0	0	0	0
-3.8	-4	-3	-4
-7.1	-8	-7	-7

The CINT(X) function rounds X to the nearest integer. However, if you need to round numbers to a prescribed number of decimal places, then the INT(X) function can be used. For example, to round X to the nearest whole number, you can write

LET R = INT(X + .5)

Note the effect of this statement on the values of X shown below.

X	X + .5	INT(X+.5)
7.2	7.7	7
7.8	8.3	8
7.5	8.0	8
7.37	7.87	7

To round to the nearest tenth, you would use the statement

LET R = INT(X * 10 + .5) / 10

The effect of this statement on various values of X follows:

X	X * 10 + .5	INT(X * 10 + .5)	INT(X * 10 + .5)/10
4.13	41.8	41	4.1
4.79	48.4	48	4.8
5.04	50.9	50	5
4.7358	47.858	47	4.7

In general, to round X to D decimal places, you can use the statement

LET R = INT(X * 10 ^ D + .5) / 10 ^ D

You should note that the equations for rounding to the nearest whole number and to the nearest tenth can be derived from this last equation by setting D to 0 and 1, respectively.

The RND Function

One of the most interesting built-in functions is the random number generator RND(X). This function generates random single-precision numbers in the range 0 to 1 exclusive. For example, the code

```
FOR I = 1 TO 10
  LET X = RND
  PRINT X
NEXT I
```

will print a sequence of 10 single-precision numbers chosen randomly by the computer. More precisely, the computer picks a seed or starting point of a sequence of random numbers when the RND function is invoked. The numbers are then generated using a fixed numerical algorithm. If this program were run repeatedly, the output would be the same sequence of numbers from the same seed. This repeated output might be useful if you needed to hold the output fixed as you debugged parts of a complicated program. In order to generate different sequences of numbers, the algorithm would require a different seed each time the program is executed. To accomplish this task, QB requires a RANDOMIZE statement before statements that include the RND function. When RANDOMIZE is used in a program, QB prompts the user for a seed by displaying the message

```
Random-number seed (-32768 to 32767)?
```

The user responds by simply choosing an integer in that range, and then the program uses that value to "seed" the RND function. If you would rather let the computer alter the seed automatically, you can use QB's TIMER function to pick the seed. (The TIMER function ties the choice of the seed to the clock of the computer.) The format of the QB statement is

```
RANDOMIZE TIMER
```

The RND function can be used with the INT(X) function to generate random integers. Integers generated randomly can be used in a wide range of applications and simulations, as you will see. Consider the following examples:

1. You want the computer to simulate the random toss of a coin. Although the computer cannot actually toss a coin, it can randomly choose between two numbers, say 0 and 1. You can then count the occurrence of 0 as the tossing of "heads" and a 1 as "tails". What statement can you use to generate random integers in the range 0 to 1? The desired statement will be developed step by step. Observe the following statements and their results:

STATEMENT	RESULT
X = RND	0 < X < 1
X = RND * 2	0 < X < 2
X = INT(RND * 2)	X = 0 or X = 1

Therefore, the last statement would be required for the coin simulation problem.

2. Suppose you want to generate random integers in the range 1 to 2. A step-by-step construction of the appropriate statement follows:

STATEMENT	RESULT
X = RND	0 < X < 1
X = RND * 2	0 < X < 2
X = INT(RND * 2)	X = 0 or X = 1
X = INT(RND * 2) + 1	X = 1 or X = 2

Thus, as you have probably observed, you only needed to add 1 to the statement in the last example to obtain the statement to generate integers randomly in the range 1 to 2.

3. Suppose you want to simulate the tossing of a single die with six faces showing the values 1 to 6. You want to program the computer to generate random integers in the range 1 to 6. Consider the following development of the appropriate statement:

STATEMENT	RESULT
X = RND	0 < X < 1
X = RND * 6	0 < X < 6
X = INT(RND * 6)	X = 0, 1, 2, 3, 4 or 5
X = INT(RND * 6) + 1	X = 1, 2, 3, 4, 5 or 6

4. Just for the fun of it, you can write a statement to generate random integers in the range 10 to 20. You have probably noticed that in the second step, RND is always multiplied by the number of possible outcomes desired. In this example, there are 11 integers in the range 10 through 20. The complete development is as follows:

STATEMENT	RESULT
X = RND	0 < X < 1
X = RND * 11	0 < X < 11
X = INT(RND * 11)	X = 0, 1, 2, ... or 10
X = INT(RND * 11) + 10	X = 10, 11, 12, ... or 20

5. As a last example, you can construct a statement to generate random integers in the range 1 to 1000. (You'll need this statement for a programming problem found at the end of this chapter.)

STATEMENT	RESULT
X = RND	0 < X < 1
X = RND * 1000	0 < X < 1000
X = INT(RND * 1000)	X = 0, 1, 2, ... or 999
X = INT(RND * 1000) + 1	X = 1, 2,3 , ... or 1000

The placement of the parentheses in the last statement in each of the above examples is very important. For example, note that the value of INT(RND) * 6 is always 0.

The next two programs show applications of the RND and INT(X) functions.

Program 20.

Step 1. Describe the problem.

A young student wants to practice elementary multiplication facts, where the factors range from 0 to 12. You want to use your newly acquired computer expertise to try your hand at computer-assisted instruction (CAI). The problem is to design a CAI program that presents 10 multiplication problems, where the integer factors are chosen randomly in the range 0 to 12. The program should tell the student if his answer is correct or not and should give the total number of problems answered correctly out of ten.

Step 2. Design the logic of the solution.

Prompts (PRINT statements) are important here to explain to the student exactly what will happen in the program. The RANDOMIZE TIMER statement is used so that a person can run the program repeatedly with a different set of questions each time. After setting a counter NCORRECT, which will keep track of correct responses, to 0, a FOR/NEXT loop is used to present the 10 problems and the immediate feedback as to the correctness of each answer. An IF...THEN statement can be used to increment the counter NCORRECT if the student's answer is correct. Then, as in any good CAI program, you can summarize the student's performance with a PRINT statement.

Step 3. Code the program.

```
REM  PROGRAM USING RND FUNCTION
PRINT "YOU WILL BE GIVEN TEN MULTIPLICATION"
PRINT "PROBLEMS, WHERE THE FACTORS RANGE FROM"
PRINT "0 THROUGH 12. PLEASE GIVE AN ANSWER FOR"
PRINT "EACH PROBLEM."
RANDOMIZE TIMER
LET NCORRECT = 0
```

```
REM ************ SELECTING THE PROBLEMS ***************
FOR I = 1 TO 10
  LET X =  INT(RND*13)
  LET Y =  INT(RND*13)
  LET ANSWER = X*Y

REM ************ ANSWERING THE PROBLEMS **************
  PRINT X;"*";Y;"="
  INPUT RESPONSE

REM ************ FEEDBACK ON RESPONSE *****************
  IF RESPONSE = ANSWER THEN
    NCORRECT = NCORRECT + 1
    PRINT "GOOD"
  ELSE
    PRINT "NOT CORRECT"
  END IF
NEXT I
PRINT "YOU ANSWERED";NCORRECT; "PROBLEMS CORRECTLY OUT OF 10."
END
```

Further Notes on Program 20:

1. It would be a simple matter to change the number of problems given or to use a range of factors other than 0 to 12 in this program. (See Review Exercise 6.)
2. Very often in a CAI lesson of this type, the user is given more than one chance to answer a problem correctly. This option is left as a programming problem.
3. The user of this program would get very tired of seeing the responses "GOOD" or "NOT CORRECT". You can vary these responses, randomly of course, from a set of eight responses very easily using the INT(X) and RND functions and the multiline IF and SELECT CASE statements. Furthermore it would be interesting to the user not only to see a score (NCORRECT) at the end of the program, but also to be ranked on the basis of this score (much like the way video games rank individuals based on number of targets hit, etc.). This option can be easily accomplished using a multiline IF statement.

To implement these enhancements to Program 20, you can modify that program with the following code. The following code would replace the FEEDBACK ON RESPONSE section in Program 20.

```
LET R = INT(RND*4) + 1
REM ****** RESPONDING TO A CORRECT ANSWER *******
IF RESPONSE = ANSWER THEN
  NCORRECT = NCORRECT + 1
  SELECT CASE R
    CASE 1
      PRINT "GOOD JOB"
    CASE 2
      PRINT "EXCELLENT"
    CASE 3
      PRINT "RIGHT!"
    CASE 4
      PRINT "CORRECT ANSWER!"
  END SELECT

REM **** RESPONDING TO AN INCORRECT ANSWER ******
ELSE
  SELECT CASE R
    CASE 1
      PRINT "NOT CORRECT"
    CASE 2
      PRINT "I DO NOT AGREE"
    CASE 3
      PRINT "CHECK THAT ONE AGAIN"
    CASE 4
      PRINT "NOT QUITE"
  END SELECT
END IF
NEXT I

REM ******* SUMMARIZING THE PERFORMANCE ***********
PRINT "YOU ANSWERED"; NCORRECT; "PROBLEMS CORRECTLY OUT OF 10."
IF NCORRECT <= 4 THEN
   PRINT "STUDY AGAIN AND TRY PROGRAM LATER."
ELSEIF NCORRECT <= 8 THEN
   PRINT "NOT BAD, TRY TO IMPROVE."
ELSE
   PRINT "WILL YOU BE A MATHEMATICIAN?"
END IF
END
```

Program 21.

Step 1. Describe the problem.

A car rental agency charges $75 per week for a particular class of car. This charge includes up to 400 miles traveled. The agency charges $.20 per mile for each additional mile or part thereof in excess of 400 miles. You want to write a QuickBASIC program that will READ miles traveled for each of 10 rentals and will calculate and print the charge for each rental.

Step 2. Design the logic of the solution.

The number of miles traveled MILES falls into one of three cases in this problem:

CASE 1: MILES <= 400. For all such rentals, the charge is $75.00.

CASE 2: MILES > 400 and MILES is an integer. In this case, the charge is $75.00 plus an additional $.20 for each mile over 400 miles, i.e. for (MILES - 400) miles. Thus, the charge is $75.00 + $.20 * (MILES - 400).

CASE 3: MILES > 400 and MILES is not an integer. The quantity MILES - 400 is also not an integer. If you take INT(MILES - 400) you certainly get an integer quantity, but you have lost the fractional part of a mile. Because, as the problem states, $.20 for any part of an additional mile must be paid, you must add 1 to INT(MILES - 400). The total cost in this case is $75.00 + $.20 * (INT(MILES - 400) + 1).

The processing of the 10 rentals can be accomplished with a FOR/NEXT loop containing a multiline IF, with data supplied through READ/DATA statements.

Step 3. Code the program.

```
REM PROGRAM TO DETERMINE CAR RENTAL COSTS WHICH
REM ARE BASED ON THE NUMBER OF MILES DRIVEN.
PRINT "RENTAL #", "MILES", "COST"
FOR RENTAL = 1 TO 10
  READ MILES
  IF MILES <= 400 THEN
    CHARGE = 75
  ELSEIF MILES = INT(MILES) THEN
    CHARGE = 75+.2*(MILES-400)
  ELSE
    CHARGE = 75+.2*(INT(MILES - 400) + 1)
  END IF
PRINT RENTAL, MILES, CHARGE
NEXT RENTAL
DATA 320, 605, 407.6, 394.2, 501
DATA 560.4, 480, 540, 402.7, 420
END
```

Output:

RENTAL #	MILES	COST
1	320	75
2	605	116
3	407.6	76.6
4	394.2	75
5	501	95.2
6	560.4	107.2
7	480	91
8	540	103
9	402.7	75.6
10	420	79

Further Notes on Program 21:

1. Cases 1, 2, and 3 described above correspond to the first, second, and third parts, respectively, of the multiline IF statement. Do you see why MILES > 400 does not need to be specified in the ELSEIF and ELSE clauses?
2. The dollar amount output in the cost column is unfortunately left justified (as usual) instead of aligned on the decimal point. Moreover, $75.60 appears as 75.6. These kinds of formatting considerations will be addressed in Chapter Six when the PRINT USING statement is discussed.

C. USER-DEFINED FUNCTIONS

QuickBASIC permits you to define your own function when you need a function that is not included in the built-in functions. There are two different formats that can be used to define functions. One form of the user-defined function is the function definition statement DEF FN, which is a single-statement function. The function definition statement has the following format:

DEF FN function name (variable list) = expression

This statement consists of four parts:

1. *DEF FN.* These letters must be part of every FunctioN DEFinition.
2. *Function Name.* The naming of the function follows the same rules as the naming of a variable (see Chapter One).
3. *Variable List.* This list contains the variables used by the function.
4. *Expression.* This is a mathematical expression involving constants and the variables in the variable list.

Consider the following example:

A function for calculating sales tax at 5% on the price of an item could be defined in a DEF FN statement and used in a PRINT statement as follows:

```
DEF FNTAX(PRICE) = PRICE * .05
      .
      .
      .
PRINT FNTAX(1000)
```

The PRINT statement invokes the function TAX and prints the value 50. Note that PRICE = 1000 in this example.

QuickBASIC also extends the user-defined function concept to a multiline form. This form, the *function procedure*, is a powerful function declaration that can accomplish everything the DEF FN can, and more. QB's function procedure is a true procedure in that it is a self-contained program unit. The format for defining a function procedure is

```
FUNCTION function name (variable list)
   statement(s)
   function name = expression
   statement(s)
END FUNCTION
```

Note that the definition of a function can include many or no statements before and after the assignment of the expression to the name of the function. Consider the following function procedure examples:

1. Suppose you want to calculate the volume of a rectangular box with length L, width W, and height H using a function procedure called VOLUME. The main program might be:

   ```
   REM FINDING THE VOLUME OF A RECTANGULAR BOX
   INPUT "ENTER DIMENSIONS";L, W, H
   PRINT VOLUME(L, W, H)
   END
   ```

   Then the function VOLUME could be written as:

   ```
   FUNCTION VOLUME (L, W, H)
     VOLUME = L * W * H
   END FUNCTION
   ```

   If you were to type in the first statement of a function procedure, the QB editor would display the function in its own window. In this way, the editor really enforces the concept that the function procedure is an independent block of code. The editor allows you to concentrate on the creation of the function without being distracted by other parts of your program. Both windows containing code are still available; you simply press Shift-F2 to toggle from one to the other. As you save your main program, all function procedures invoked by that program are also saved. Moreover, the editor adds a DECLARE FUNCTION statement to the main program. Note that in the above example, as is the case whenever functions are invoked, the function returns a single value to the main program.

2. User-defined functions and built-in functions can be incorporated into the same QB statement. If VOLUME was previously defined, the following statement could be evaluated:

```
LET A = SQR(X) + INT(Y) + VOLUME(10, 20, 30)
```

3. You can write a function procedure to calculate the charge in the car rental example, Program 21. Using the three cases as described for assigning a charge, you could write the following function:

```
FUNCTION CHARGE(MILES)
  IF MILES <= 400 THEN
    CHARGE = 75
  ELSEIF MILES = INT(MILES) THEN
    CHARGE = 75 + .2 * (MILES-400)
  ELSE
    CHARGE = 75 + .2 * (INT(MILES-400)+1)
  END IF
END FUNCTION
```

The main program would then be simplified considerably as follows:

```
REM CAR RENTAL PROBLEM
PRINT "RENTAL","MILES","COST"
FOR RENTAL = 1 TO 10
  READ MILES
  PRINT RENTAL,MILES,CHARGE(MILES)
NEXT RENTAL
DATA 320, 605, 407.6, 394.2, 501
DATA 560.4, 480, 540, 402.7, 420
END
```

Note that the use of the function procedure makes the main program seem easy. The invocation of the function CHARGE simply appears as part of a PRINT statement. A person viewing the code for the first time can easily see what the program is to accomplish. Once the main program is understood, the person could then review the procedure that calculates the charge to get all the details. In this way, the modular approach leads to a more understandable, structured QB program.

The following program uses a function procedure.

Program 22.

Step 1. Describe the problem.

You want to write a money changer program that determines the number of each specific type of currency (dollars, quarters, dimes, nickels, and pennies) to be given as change from the sale of an item. The input will be the price of the item and the amount tendered by the customer. The output will be a listing of the change to be given.

Step 2. Design the logic of the solution.

The PRICE and the AMOUNT tendered will be entered without decimal points to allow simpler expressions in the function definitions. You will then define a function to determine the number of dollars, quarters, dimes, and nickels to be given as change. For example, suppose PRICE is subtracted from AMOUNT to find that CHANGE is equal to 467. Then, to determine the number of dollars to be given as change, you need a function that would use the expression INT(CHANGE / 100). Because INT(467 / 100) = 4, this expression has determined that four dollar bills should be part of the change given to the customer. After subtracting 400 from 467, the remaining change, namely 67, will be routed through the function several more times to determine the number of quarters, dimes, and nickels to be given as change. Note that you'll need to change the denominator in the expression from 100 to 25, 10, and 5 to obtain the correct amount of change. When all of the calculations have been completed, the amount of change in dollars, quarters, dimes, nickels, and pennies will be printed.

Step 3. Code the program.

```
REM  MONEY CHANGER PROGRAM.  EACH FUNCTION
REM  DETERMINES THE NUMBER OF A
REM  SPECIFIC TYPE OF CURRENCY TO BE
REM  GIVEN AS CHANGE FROM THE SALE OF AN ITEM.

REM ****** ENTERING PRICE AND AMOUNT TENDERED *******
INPUT "ENTER PRICE OF ITEM, WITHOUT DECIMAL POINT"; PRICE
INPUT "ENTER AMOUNT TENDERED, WITHOUT DECIMAL POINT"; AMOUNT

REM ********** CALCULATING THE CHANGE ****************
IF AMOUNT > PRICE THEN
  CHANGE = AMOUNT - PRICE
  DOLLAR = CHANGER(CHANGE, 100)
  CHANGE = CHANGE - DOLLAR * 100
  QUARTER = CHANGER(CHANGE, 25)
  CHANGE = CHANGE - QUARTER * 25
  DIME = CHANGER(CHANGE, 10)
  CHANGE = CHANGE - DIME * 10
  NICKEL = CHANGER(CHANGE, 5)
  CHANGE = CHANGE - NICKEL * 5
  PRINT

  REM ****** PRINTING OUT THE CHANGE REQUIRED ********
  PRINT "THE AMOUNT OF CHANGE IS"
  PRINT
  PRINT DOLLAR; "DOLLARS"
  PRINT QUARTER; "QUARTERS"
  PRINT DIME; "DIMES"
  PRINT NICKEL; "NICKELS"
  PRINT CHANGE; "PENNIES"
ELSE
```

```
  PRINT ''ERROR''
END IF
END

FUNCTION CHANGER (CHANGE, CURRENCY)
  CHANGER = INT(CHANGE/CURRENCY)
END FUNCTION
```

Sample output:

```
ENTER PRICE OF ITEM, WITHOUT DECIMAL POINT? 427
ENTER AMOUNT TENDERED, WITHOUT DECIMAL POINT? 1000

THE AMOUNT OF CHANGE IS

 5 DOLLARS
 2 QUARTERS
 2 DIMES
 0 NICKELS
 3 PENNIES
```

Further Notes on Program 22:

1. The IF statement checks if the customer tendered enough money for the purchase. If not, an error message is printed.
2. Note that the two parameters, CHANGE and CURRENCY, passed to the function are in a specific order.
3. An additional invocation of the function CHANGER to calculate the number of pennies is not necessary, because this quantity is already determined in the statement CHANGE = CHANGE - NICKEL * 5.
4. Note that DOLLAR is the variable name whose value is the number of dollars of change to be given, whereas ''DOLLARS'' is a character string constant. Similarly, the statements for the other monetary amounts each contain a variable followed by a string constant.

D. SUBROUTINES

A *subroutine* is a sequence of program statements designed to perform a specific task. This set of statements may be called for execution from several points within the program. Thus, instead of a program having several sequences of redundant code, it uses one set of code repeatedly. Control can transfer from the main program to the subroutine and back again as often as needed. Subroutines are usually placed at the end of the program. The important statements in QuickBASIC to facilitate the program flow with subroutines are the GOSUB and RETURN statements.

The GOSUB Statement

The GOSUB statement causes an unconditional branch to a subroutine. Subroutines must be called using this statement. The format is

GOSUB label or line #

where the label or line number in this statement indicates the first statement of the subroutine. The label or line number must always be followed by a colon(:). The computer stores in memory which GOSUB statement in a program has been executed most recently. In this way, the program is able to transfer control back to the appropriate statement once the subroutine has been executed.

The RETURN statement

The last executable statement in a subroutine is always a RETURN statement. This statement transfers control back to the "main program" by causing a branch back to the line after the GOSUB that (most recently) called the subroutine. Its format is

RETURN

Because this statement will transfer control to different locations in a program if the subroutine is used more than once, no line number or label is placed after the word RETURN.

As an example, consider Figure 3.2, where a subroutine CALCULATIONS is to be called twice after entering data in a program. The numbers in parentheses in this figure indicate the sequence of branching that takes place in this program. When GOSUB CALCULATIONS is executed the first time, a branch to the subroutine occurs. After the subroutine is executed, control transfers to the line after the one that called the subroutine, namely, PRINT VALUE. Then lines of the program are executed in sequence until the second GOSUB is reached, at which point a branch to the subroutine occurs again. After the subroutine is executed a second time, control transfers to the INPUT statement. The execution of statements then continues to the END of the program. You are encouraged to study the program flow (as indicated by the numbers in parentheses) in this diagram.

Program 23.

Program 17 contained a menu from which a user could select an arithmetic operation to be performed on numbers entered at the terminal. The menu was printed only once, even though the user could select a sequence of operations to be performed. It would be helpful to repeat the menu selection, because the menu soon disappears due to the scrolling of the output screen. Without the use of a subroutine, you would have to duplicate the nine PRINT statements that display the menu. Instead, however, you can place those statements in a subroutine that can be called when needed. Program 23 contains a menu subroutine as well as a subroutine to perform the appropriate arithmetic operation based on the user's menu selection.

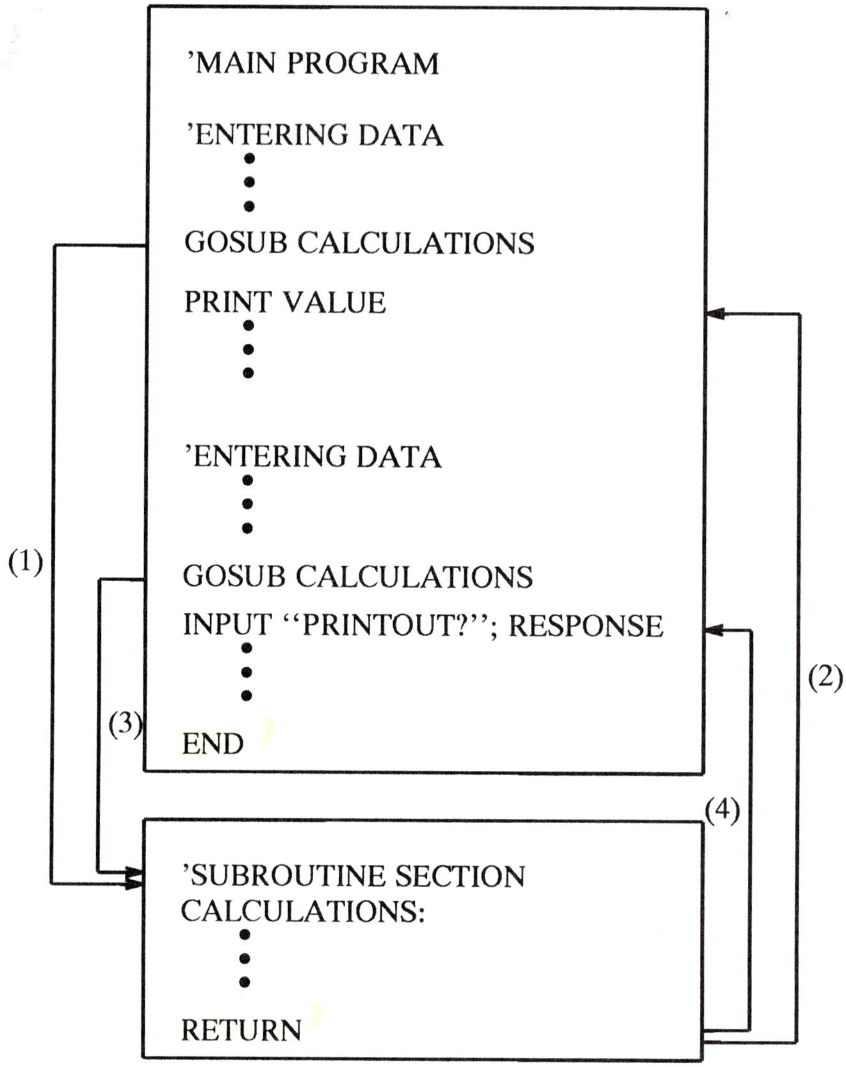

Figure 3.2. Program Flow with a Subroutine

```
REM ***** ARITHMETIC OPERATIONS MAIN PROGRAM *******
GOSUB MENU
IF CHOICE < > 5 THEN INPUT ''ENTER TWO NUMBERS'';X, Y
WHILE CHOICE < > 5
  GOSUB ARITHMETIC
  GOSUB MENU
WEND
PRINT ''HOPE YOU HAD FUN!''
END
REM  ********SUBROUTINES FOLLOW**************
```

```
REM ******* SELECTING FROM A MENU **********
MENU:
PRINT “CHOOSE ONE OF THE FOLLOWING:”
PRINT
PRINT “1. ADDITION”
PRINT “2. SUBTRACTION”
PRINT “3. MULTIPLICATION”
PRINT “4. DIVISION”
PRINT “5. END THE PROGRAM”
PRINT
INPUT “ENTER 1, 2, 3, 4, OR 5:”;CHOICE
RETURN

REM ******** PROCESSING THE CHOICE **********
ARITHMETIC:
SELECT CASE CHOICE
  CASE 1
    PRINT X;“+”;Y;“=”;X + Y
  CASE 2
    PRINT X;“-”;Y;“=”;X - Y
  CASE 3
    PRINT X;“*”;Y;“=”;X * Y
  CASE 4
    PRINT X;“/”;Y;“=”;X / Y
  CASE ELSE
    REM THIS BLOCK HELPS TO PREVENT ERROR MESSAGES
END SELECT
PRINT
RETURN
```

A Further Note on Program 23:

The menu of arithmetic operations is now displayed each time a CHOICE needs to be made. Once again, only if CHOICE is *not* 5 will the user be asked to enter two numbers.

E. QUICKBASIC SUBPROGRAMS

QuickBASIC contains another type of procedure in addition to the user-defined function called the *subprogram*. Like function procedures, these are independent sets of code designed to facilitate structured programming and a modular approach to software development. Although subprograms and their powerful features are beyond the scope of this text, if you are interested in them, you are encouraged to consult a QB reference manual for the details.

F. REVIEW EXERCISES

1. Write a QuickBASIC assignment statement that returns a random integer X in the range
   (a) 0 through 3,
   (b) 2 through 14,
   (c) -10 through +10.

2. Show the output of the following programs.

(a)
```
LET X = 11
WHILE X < > SQR(X)
  PRINT X; INT(SQR(X))
  IF X / 2 = INT(X / 2) THEN X = X / 2 ELSE X = X - 1
WEND
PRINT "DONE"
END
```

(b)
```
DEF FNA(X) = X + 10
DEF FNB(X) = X + 5
L = 5
FOR I = 1 TO 3
  L = FNA(L) - FNB(L) + L
  PRINT L
NEXT I
END
```

(c)
```
FOR I = 1 TO 3
   READ X, Y
   GOSUB PRINTVALUE
NEXT I
DATA 3, 5, 8
DATA 6, -2, 1
END
PRINTVALUE:
PRINT I;X;Y;X + Y
RETURN
```

3. Write a user-defined function called P that calculates the perimeter of a rectangle (the distance around the rectangle) with width W and length L. (Example: the distance around a rectangle with W = 2 and L = 5 is 14; i.e., 2*W + 2*L.)

4. Program 21 contains a statement to determine if MILES is an integer. Write a similar statement that determines if a number N is even or odd.

5. Write a statement that will round a value X to the nearest
   (a) hundredth
   (b) thousandth.

6. Modify Program 20 so that 20 multiplication problems are presented with factors ranging from 0 to 15.

G. LAB EXERCISES

1. Enter and run this program:

```
REM MAKE A TABLE OF SQUARE ROOTS
PRINT "NUMBER","SQUARE ROOT"
FOR NUMBER = 1 TO 25
  PRINT NUMBER, SQR(NUMBER)
NEXT NUMBER
END
```

   Which statement "invokes" a function? What is the function?

   ____

   How can you tell if a function is in a program?

   ____

   How many values does the function return?

   ____

2. You can write your own functions so that calculations you need to perform over and over can be accomplished by invoking the function with the correct arguments instead of rewriting all the statements again. As an example, start by entering and executing this program.

```
REM PROGRAM TO PRINT A SERIES OF NUMBERS
RANDOMIZE TIMER
CLS
PRINT "WELCOME TO THE CRAZY NUMBERS PRINTING PROGRAM"
PRINT "YOU WILL SEE THE NUMBERS IN THE SEQUENCE COME UP RAN-
DOMLY"
PRINT
PRINT
PRINT "SELECT ONE OF THE FOLLOWING:"
PRINT
PRINT "1. NUMBERS 1,2,3,4"
PRINT "2. NUMBERS 1,2,3,4,5,6"
PRINT "3. NUMBERS 1,2,3,4,5,6,7,8"
PRINT "4. YOUR OWN SEQUENCE"
```

```
PRINT
PRINT "INPUT 1,2,3, OR 4"
INPUT SELECTION
SELECT CASE SELECTION
CASE 1
REM THE NUMBERS 1 THROUGH 4
FOR I = 1 TO 10
   X = INT(RND * 4) + 1
   PRINT X;" ";
NEXT I
CASE 2
REM THE NUMBERS 1 THROUGH 6
FOR I = 1 TO 10
   X = INT(RND * 6) + 1
   PRINT X;" ";
NEXT I
CASE 3
REM THE NUMBERS 1 THROUGH 8
FOR I = 1 TO 10
   X = INT(RND * 8) + 1
   PRINT X;" ";
NEXT I
CASE 4
REM USER'S OWN SELECTION
PRINT "ENTER THE BEGINNING NUMBER OF THE SERIES"
INPUT FIRST
PRINT "ENTER THE FINAL NUMBER OF THE SERIES"
INPUT LAST
IF INT(FIRST) > INT(LAST) THEN
   PRINT "SORRY, THE FIRST NUMBER FOR WHICH YOU ENTERED";FIRST
   PRINT "MUST BE LESS THAN THE FINAL NUMBER FOR WHICH YOU
ENTERED";LAST
ELSE
   RANGE = INT(LAST) - INT(FIRST) + 1
   FOR I = 1 TO 10
      X = INT(RND * RANGE) + INT(FIRST)
      PRINT X;" ";
   NEXT I
END IF
END SELECT
PRINT
END
```

What happens when you enter a 1 for the above program?

____

What happens when you enter a 2?

What happens when you enter a 3?

What happens when you enter a 4?

Now enter the number 3 for the prompt "Input the beginning number of the series" and the number 6 for the prompt "Input the final number of the series" What happens?

Run selection 4 again with the numbers -1 and -6. Results?

Run selection 4 with the numbers -9 and -6. Results?

Why is the INT function used in the statement RANGE=INT(LAST)-INT(FIRST)+1?

What if you really wanted to see the series from a negative number to a positive number generated (for example, the series -3 to 3; i.e., the numbers -3, -2, -1, 0, 1, 2, 3)? Can it be done?

Notice in this program that you need four different ranges of random numbers! It would make sense to have a general function of your own to do this calculation and use it where it is needed. You can add the following function definition to the program immediately following the statement RANDOMIZE TIMER.

DEF FNRANDOMNUM(RANGE, SHIFTFACTOR) = INT(RND * RANGE) + SHIFT-FACTOR

Notice that this user-defined function gives you a general way of finding the number RANGE. It uses the parameters of RANGE and SHIFTFACTOR. Remember that the term *range* refers to the number of different values you want to produce. Some examples are

1,2,3,4	four numbers; thus the range is 4
6,7,8	three numbers; thus the range is 3
4,5,6,7,8,9	six numbers; thus the range is 6

The SHIFTFACTOR determines the starting number in the RANGE. Using the above example, the SHIFTFACTORS are 1,6, and 4, respectively.

Now you can see that different parameters supplied to the function RANDOMNUM will produce different ranges. Using the above function, if you wanted to produce the sequence 1,2,3,4,5,6,7, you would assign a value of 7 to the RANGE and a value of 1 to the SHIFTFACTOR. Thus the statement used in the program that gives these values is

```
FNRANDOMNUM(7,1)
```

Notice that 7 is the RANGE, because it is listed first, and 1 is the SHIFTFACTOR, because it is the second parameter of the function.

Now look at the program again. Rewrite these lines in the program that can use the function FNRANDOMNUM

Without the Function	*With the Function*
X = INT(RND*4) + 1	
X = INT(RND*6) + 1	
X = INT(RND*8) + 1	
X = INT(RND*RANGE) + INT(FIRST)	

Run the program again, this time with the new function. Does it make a difference in the execution?

____

3. The key idea when using subroutines is to break up a program into intellectually manageable as well as reusable pieces. Lets take a closer look at the program. Notice how the following code is repeated in each of our selections:

```
FOR I = 1 to 10
   find the random number
   print the random number
NEXT I
```

It would be better to identify these lines as a subroutine and call it when you need it. Notice that you then have only one set of statements that will look like the above, instead of four.

Here is the subroutine.

```
REM START OF THE SUBROUTINE
PRINTNUMBERS:
   FOR I = 1 TO 10
      X = FNRANDOMNUM(RANGE, SHIFTFACTOR)
      PRINT X;" ";
   NEXT I
RETURN
```

Notice that the subroutine is placed just after the END statement. This is the normal location for subroutines.

Now replace the lines in the program with the new lines that use the subroutine. Notice that the subroutine uses the variables RANGE and SHIFTFACTOR. This implies that these variables must be defined *before* you transfer control to the subroutine. Thus the replacement lines are as follows:

```
RANGE = _______
SHIFTFACTOR = ________
GOSUB PRINTNUMBERS
```

Now modify the appropriate parts and run this program. Do these changes make a difference in the execution?

____

Do these changes make a difference in the logic of the program?

____

H. PROGRAMMING PROBLEMS

1. In Program 20, the student is given one chance to enter the correct answer to each multiplication problem. Rewrite this program so that if the student answers incorrectly on the first try, he or she is given a second chance to enter the correct answer.

2. Write a program that simulates the tossing of a single coin 500 times. The output should consist of the number of times "heads" and "tails" occurs.

3. (a) Suppose gambling is legal in your town and you would like to play a dice game in the local casino. The game is simple: a regular die is rolled and players bet on numbers 1 through 6. If you bet \$1 on a number, you win \$5 (a net gain of \$4) if that number comes up. Write a program that simulates 500 rolls in the game. Pick one of the numbers 1 through 6 as your lucky number. The output should show how many times you would have won or lost and your net after 500 bets.

   (b) Play the game with an 8-sided die, with the player betting on the numbers 1 through 8, winning \$8 (net gain of \$7) on a \$1 bet. The output should again show how many times you would have won or lost and your net after 500 bets.

4. As a result of your newly acquired expertise in computer programming, you have accepted a summer job with a company specializing in the development of computer games. Your first assignment on the job is to write a QuickBASIC program that plays the game "GUESS MY NUMBER." The program is to set up an interaction between the computer and a player at a terminal.

   The program should choose the number to be guessed by selecting an integer at random in the range 1 to 1000. The player then sees the prompt:

```
MY NUMBER IS BETWEEN 1 AND 1000.
GUESS IT IF YOU CAN.
```

After the player enters his guess, he sees either the message

WOW! YOU GUESSED THE NUMBER!
DO YOU WANT TO PLAY AGAIN?
PLEASE TYPE "YES" OR "NO".

or

YOUR GUESS IS TOO LOW. TRY AGAIN.

or

YOUR GUESS IS TOO HIGH. TRY AGAIN.

The program should allow the player 15 attempts to guess the number and should keep telling the player whether he is too high or too low to help him "find" the number. If 15 incorrect guesses are entered, the program should display the secret number. (If the player uses the correct strategy, he will always be able to find the number in 10 or fewer tries.)

Your program should allow the user to play the game more than once. When the player indicates that he no longer wishes to play, your program should cause an appropriate signoff message to appear as output to indicate that the game is over.

5. Modify the program you have written for Problem 4 above so that the introduction and the signoff message are printed in subroutines.

6. In this problem you will use QuickBASIC's random number generator to write a program to play a game of "sea battle." In this game, there is an enemy submarine hidden in a 10 x 10 grid-like area, where (0,0) is at the lower-left corner. The submarine will occupy ONLY ONE grid location. The user is the captain of a battleship that fires upon the sub by entering a pair of coordinates that is assumed to be the location of the sub. The program then responds with the results of the shot (hit or miss).

   Your program should use the RND and INT functions to "hide" the submarine in a random location within the 10 x 10 area. Then allow the user to guess the coordinates of the sub's position. If the user guesses correctly, print an appropriate message. Otherwise, print a message telling the user where the shot fell in relation to the sub (north, south, east, west, northeast, etc.). The user should be allowed three or five tries before the sub retaliates and sinks the battleship. Use the RND function to determine how many (three or five) guesses the user gets for each "battle" (there should be a 50% chance of either number of shots). Your program should also allow the user to play more than once. When the user no longer wishes to play, your program should print a signoff message stating that the battle is over.

   Follow these guidelines in writing your program:

   (a) Be sure to include the RANDOMIZE statement in your program so that you'll get random results.

   (b) Print a header to introduce the battle (e.g., *Somewhere in a 10 x 10 area lurks an enemy sub. You have five tries to sink it before it sinks you!*).

(c) For each guess, print the guess number and then ask for a pair of coordinates from the user. If the guess is incorrect, print something to the effect of

Shot fell <direction> of the sub,

where <direction> is one of north, south, east, west, northeast, etc. You must use a series of IF...THEN statements to do this, where the conditions compare the coordinates entered with the actual location of the sub. For example, if the sub is at position (3,4) and the user guesses (7,6), then the shot fell *northeast* of the sub, because 7 is above or *north* of 3 and 6 is is to the right or *east* of 4. (If you need to, draw a picture to convince yourself that this is the case.)

(d) If the user runs out of guesses, print where the sub was hidden.

CHAPTER FOUR

ARRAYS

"*There was an old woman who lived in a shoe, she had so many children she didn't know what to do.*" (Nursery rhyme, earliest known version, 1797.)

A. INTRODUCTION

This chapter begins with a story.

Mom's Rentals

This story is about a lady who lived in a large house near a university campus. One year, to earn a little extra income, she rented a spare room in the house to a college student. She found that being a landlady was, more often than not, a pleasant experience. As her own children grew up and moved out of the house, two more rooms became available. The lady decided to rent these rooms, too, and she formulated a simple numbering system to help in her record keeping. The rooms would be numbered 1, 2, and 3 and on paper she could keep track of the monthly income for each room.

As the years passed, renters found this lady to be a fair and reasonable landlady. The students called her Mom and the house was known as Mom's Rentals. Mom also enjoyed the success of her rental business and one day decided to add rooms onto the house to expand her enterprise. The new rooms were numbered 4, 5, 6, ... 20.

At times, Mom would be inundated with paperwork. After all, it was hard to keep track of the monthly rents for each of the 20 rooms. So she decided to ask one of her renters, who incidentally had read the first four chapters of this very book, if a computer would be a useful tool for her record keeping. She thought that it would be just wonderful if the computer could somehow store the rents for each of the 20 rooms. Now Mom knew that she didn't want 20 different variable names. That just seemed too cumbersome. What she wanted was only one name to remember, say R, for rooms.

Her renter just smiled when he heard her request, because he knew exactly what she needed. He knew of a memory structure that could be referenced by a single name R and yet have 20 (or more) individual cells that would act as 20 (or more) different variables. He told

Mom about arrays.

B. ONE-DIMENSIONAL ARRAYS

An *array* is a group of consecutive memory locations referenced by a single name. (Array names must adhere to the same rules as variable names.) The individual cells in the array are numbered by a subscript corresponding to their position in the array. You can refer to an individual storage location by specifying its position in the array. For example, for an array named A with 10 cells, the subscripted names of each of the positions are as follows:

$$A_1, A_2, A_3, \ldots A_{10} .$$

Because subscripts cannot be typed in a program, the following notation is used to denote these same cells:

A(1), A(2), A(3), ... A(10) .

An array is not automatically available in a program. You need to specifically identify and dimension all arrays to be used. (In some versions of BASIC, arrays with 10 or fewer cells are automatically established.) This is done with the DIM statement, which has the following format:

DIM list of array names and lengths

Some examples follow.

1. The following DIM statement establishes a numerical array N of 50 cells.

   DIM N(50)

2. Mom might use the next statement to establish a numerical array R with 20 cells:

   DIM R(20)

3. To create a numerical array ITEMS with 50 cells and a numerical array PARTS with 400 cells, you could use the single statement

   DIM ITEMS(50), PARTS(400)

4. To create a character string array PERSON$ with 50 cells and a numerical array SCORE with 50 cells, you could use the single statement

   DIM PERSON$(50), SCORE(50)

Mom's array R with 20 cells can be pictured as shown in Figure 4.1. Each of the cells is identified by a room number in the range from 1 to 20. The contents of each memory location is the rent for that room for a given month. Since R(1) is 125, this means that room 1 rents for $125 per month. Since R(2) is 140, room 2 rents for $140 per month, and so on.

125	140	140		0	100	125
R(1)	R(2)	R(3)	. . .	R(18)	R(19)	R(20)

Figure 4.1. A Diagram of a 20-Element Array in Memory

Mom's Rentals will be referred to several more times in this chapter as applications of arrays are developed.

Handling Data in Arrays

How are data assigned to cells in an array and how can values in an array be printed out? These tasks are easily accomplished with FOR/NEXT loops because the initial and limit value in the FOR statement can be simply the first and last subscript used to identify array cells. For example, if Mom wanted to enter rent values into R(1) through R(20) using READ/DATA statements, she could use the following program segment:

```
FOR I = 1 TO 20
  READ R(I)
NEXT I
DATA 125, 140, 140, 100, 0, 150, 120, 110, 110, 100
DATA 90, 110, 130, 100, 110, 100, 80, 0, 100, 125
```

Printing out these values is even easier:

```
FOR I = 1 TO 20
  PRINT R(I)
NEXT I
```

Note that in the above code the subscript is given by the variable I. Any legal numerical expression can be used to denote the subscript.

The next program uses an array to print out 20 scores and their average.

Program 24.

```
REM READ IN AND PRINT OUT SCORES AND AVERAGE
CLS
DIM SCORE(20)
SUM = 0
FOR I = 1 TO 20
  READ SCORE(I)
  PRINT SCORE(I);
  SUM = SUM + SCORE(I)
NEXT I
AVE = SUM / 20
PRINT
PRINT "AVERAGE OF THE SCORES IS"; AVE
```

```
DATA 75, 100, 80, 90, 92, 94, 68, 70, 81, 92
DATA 48, 99, 100, 80, 68, 55, 79, 87, 90, 94
END
```

Output:

75 100 80 90 92 94 68 70 81 92 48 99 100 80 68 55 79 87 90 94

AVERAGE OF SCORES IS 82.1

A Further Note on Program 24:

You will recognize that this same task can be accomplished without using an array. For example, the FOR/NEXT loop can be written as

```
FOR I = 1 TO 20
  READ SCORE
  PRINT SCORE;
  SUM = SUM + SCORE
NEXT I
```

However, there is one significant difference here. After this loop is executed, only the last value of SCORE is available for further processing (if needed). When using the array SCORE, all 20 values still reside in memory and can be used again after the statement NEXT I if needed in the program. For example, suppose that after the average is calculated, you want to print out each score and a message as to how much each score is above or below the average. Without the use of an array, you would need to RESTORE the data and then read all the values again from the data statements. However, using the array SCORE, you could simply add the following lines to accomplish this task:

```
FOR I = 1 TO 20
  IF SCORE(I)>AVE THEN
    PRINT SCORE(I);"IS ABOVE AVERAGE BY";SCORE(I)-AVE
  ELSEIF SCORE(I)<AVE THEN
    PRINT SCORE(I);"IS BELOW AVERAGE BY";AVE-SCORE(I)
  ELSE
    PRINT SCORE(I);"IS EQUAL TO THE AVERAGE"
  END IF
NEXT I
```

The next program segment fills three small arrays. A diagram of the contents of these arrays is given in Figure 4.2.

```
DIM N$(4), D(4), E(4)
FOR I = 1 TO 4
```

```
  READ N$(I), D(I), E(I)
NEXT I
DATA JANE,1,2,JOHN,4,5
DATA SAM,7,8,CLYDE,11,12
```

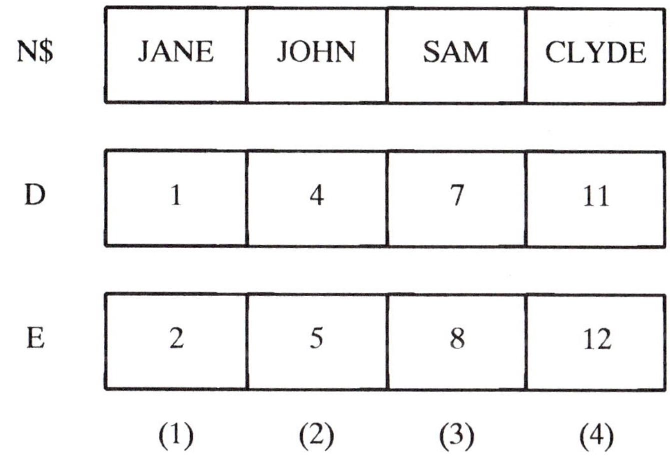

Figure 4.2. A Schematic Diagram of the Arrays N$, D, and E

Array elements can appear singly in a program just as common variables do. The following are some examples of array elements used in assignment statements and in an IF...THEN statement.

Statement	Meaning
X = Y(8)	The value in the eighth cell of the array Y is assigned to X.
A$(25) = B$(21)	The string in the twenty-first cell of array B$ is assigned to the twenty-fifth cell in array A$.
L(21) = 7	The twenty-first cell in array L is given the value 7.
IF Y(11) = 27 THEN ...	If the eleventh cell in array Y has the value 27 then ... .

Some advantages of using arrays are the following. Arrays

(1) reduce the number of "different" variable names required in a program,

(2) relate under one name quantities of the same type,

(3) allow quick storage and retrieval of data through FOR/NEXT loops,

(4) allow data to be referred to repeatedly in a program without rereading (as mentioned in the discussion after Program 24),

(5) facilitate easy manipulation of data, including merges, searches, and sorts. (You will see an example of a sort in this chapter, and examples of a search appear in Chapter Five, Programming Problem 5, and again in Chapter Seven, Program 40.)

Now for more examples showing the versatility and power of arrays.

Program 25.

Step 1. Describe the problem.

There is a new hamburger place in town called Dumpy's Burgers. After a few weeks in business, the owners take a poll where N people are asked to rate their dumpy-burger on a scale of 1 to 10. You have been consulted to write a computer program to summarize the results of the poll. The input will consist of N numbers in the range 1 to 10. The output will be the frequency of each response.

Step 2. Design the logic of the solution.

You can use an array called RATING with 10 cells that will hold the frequency, or count, of each of the possible ratings 1 through 10. In other words, the contents of RATING(1) (remember, RATING(1) is the first cell in the array RATING) is the number of times a rating of 1 is given, RATING(2) contains the number of times the response 2 is given, and so on. The responses are collected at the end of the day and entered into the program in DATA lines. You only need to know the number N of responses given. (In the example, N = 50.) As a response is read in, the appropriate cell RATING(RESPONSE) in the array is incremented by 1. After all of the responses are tabulated, the results are printed with appropriate headings.

Step 3. Code the program.

```
REM  THIS PROGRAM COUNTS RESPONSES TO A POLL WHERE N
REM  PEOPLE ARE SURVEYED AND GIVE A RANKING OF 1 TO 10.
DIM RATING(10)

REM ***** INITIALIZING THE ARRAY *************
FOR I = 1 TO 10
  LET RATING(I) = 0
NEXT I

REM ***** TOTALING THE RESPONSES ************
READ N
FOR I = 1  TO N
  READ RESPONSE
  RATING(RESPONSE) = RATING(RESPONSE) + 1
NEXT I

REM ***** PRINTING THE RESULTS ***************
PRINT "RESPONSE", "FREQUENCY"
FOR RESPONSE = 1 TO 10
 PRINT RESPONSE, RATING(RESPONSE)
NEXT RESPONSE
DATA 50
```

```
DATA 1, 4, 2, 5, 3, 6, 5, 8, 9, 3, 6, 2, 7, 3, 10, 5, 4, 7, 3, 8, 1, 9, 1, 10, 1
DATA 7, 3, 8, 4, 6, 1, 4, 6, 2, 3, 7, 9, 5, 8, 4, 10, 5, 2, 6, 3, 8, 4, 6, 2, 1
END
```

Output:

```
RESPONSE   FREQUENCY
  1           6
  2           5
  3           7
  4           6
  5           5
  6           6
  7           4
  8           5
  9           3
  10          3
```

Further Notes on Program 25:

1. DATA lines could easily be added to this program to accommodate more rankings. The only other change required would be a modification of the statement DATA 50.
2. Note that the first FOR/NEXT loop initializes all ten counters to 0. In QuickBASIC, array cells are automatically set to 0. However, just as with simple summing variables, it is a good programming practice to initialize these array cells to 0.

Program 26.

Step 1. Describe the problem.

You want to write a program that fills the arrays FIRST containing 15 cells and SECOND with 20 cells and then checks for matching numbers in the arrays. The numbers are entered from the terminal and the output will consist of the numbers appearing in both arrays.

Step 2. Design the logic of the solution.

Because the arrays are of different sizes, you will use two FOR/NEXT loops, one with limit value 15 and the other with limit value 20, to fill the arrays. To find matches, you will use nested loops to implement the following strategy. Let I control the subscripting in array FIRST and J represent the subscripts in SECOND, as depicted in Figure 4.3. Then, when I = 1, compare FIRST(1) to SECOND(1). If a match occurs, print that value and increment I to 2 to compare FIRST(2) to values in SECOND. If FIRST(1) ≠ SECOND(1), then compare FIRST(1) to SECOND(2), SECOND(3), and so on (as depicted by the arrows in Figure 4.3). If no match occurs after 20 comparisons, increment I and compare this next entry in array FIRST to SECOND(1), SECOND(2) ... as before.

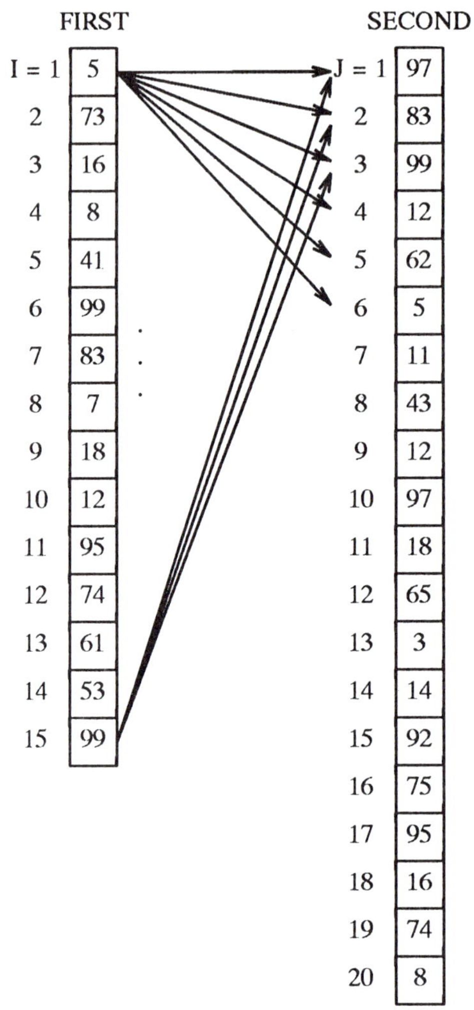

Figure 4.3. Finding Matching Numbers in Arrays

Step 3. Code the program.

```
REM  PROGRAM TO READ 15 NUMBERS INTO ARRAY FIRST,
REM  20 NUMBERS INTO ARRAY SECOND AND CHECK FOR MATCHES
DIM FIRST(15), SECOND(20)

REM ******** FILLING THE ARRAYS *********************
PRINT "FILLING FIRST ARRAY."
FOR I = 1 TO 15
  INPUT FIRST(I)
NEXT I
PRINT "NOW FILLING SECOND ARRAY."
FOR I = 1 TO 20
  INPUT SECOND(I)
NEXT I
```

```
REM ********* FINDING MATCHES ************************
FOR I = 1 TO 15
 J = 1
 EQUAL = 0
 WHILE J <= 20 AND NOT(EQUAL = 1)
  IF FIRST(I) = SECOND(J) THEN EQUAL = 1
  J = J+1
 WEND
 IF EQUAL = 1 THEN PRINT FIRST(I);"IS IN BOTH ARRAYS"
NEXT I
END
```

Further Notes on Program 26:

1. This program does not identify when a number in array FIRST appears more than once in array SECOND.
2. A number appearing twice in FIRST and once in SECOND would be printed twice.
3. The variable EQUAL is used to determine if a match has been found. EQUAL is 0 when no match is found, and EQUAL is set to 1 when a match occurs.
4. When a match is found, the value printed, FIRST(I), can be replaced by SECOND(J).
5. Modifications of this program are considered in Review Exercises 7 and 8.

Program 27.

Step 1. Describe the problem.

You want to write a program that prints out all two-letter combinations of the alphabet that have exactly one vowel (A, E, I, O, U, Y) and one consonant. For the purpose of this program, consider a pair such as AB different from BA so that both pairs are to be printed.

Step 2. Design the logic of the solution.

Dimension two arrays CONSONANT$(20) and VOWEL$(6) to hold the two sets of character strings. (Of course, each string contains only a single character.) Use a FOR/NEXT loop with a READ statement to fill each of these arrays. To print all of the combinations, A is matched with each consonant, then E is matched with each consonant, and so forth. This strategy suggests a nested loop to generate all of the two-letter combinations of the entries in the two arrays.

Step 3. Code the program.

```
REM  PROGRAM THAT PRINTS ALL TWO-LETTER
REM  COMBINATIONS OF A VOWEL AND A CONSONANT
DIM CONSONANT$(20), VOWEL$(6)
```

```
REM ******* FILLING THE ARRAYS *******************
FOR I = 1 TO 6
  READ VOWEL$(I)
NEXT I
FOR I = 1 TO 20
  READ CONSONANT$(I)
NEXT I

REM ******* PRINTING TWO-LETTER COMBINATIONS ******
FOR I = 1 TO 20
  FOR J = 1 TO 6
    PRINT CONSONANT$(I); VOWEL$(J); " "; VOWEL$(J); CONSONANT$(I);" ";
  NEXT J
  PRINT
NEXT I
DATA A, E, I, O, U, Y
DATA B, C, D, F, G, H, J, K, L, M, N, P, Q, R, S, T, V, W, X, Z
END
```

Output:

```
BA  AB  BE  EB  BI  IB  BO  OB  BU  UB  BY  YB
CA  AC  CE  EC  CI  IC  CO  OC  CU  UC  CY  YC
DA  AD  DE  ED  DI  ID  DO  OD  DU  UD  DY  YD
FA  AF  FE  EF  FI  IF  FO  OF  FU  UF  FY  YF
GA  AG  GE  EG  GI  IG  GO  OG  GU  UG  GY  YG
HA  AH  HE  EH  HI  IH  HO  OH  HU  UH  HY  YH
JA  AJ  JE  EJ  JI  IJ  JO  OJ  JU  UJ  JY  YJ
KA  AK  KE  EK  KI  IK  KO  OK  KU  UK  KY  YK
LA  AL  LE  EL  LI  IL  LO  OL  LU  UL  LY  YL
MA  AM  ME  EM  MI  IM  MO  OM  MU  UM  MY  YM
NA  AN  NE  EN  NI  IN  NO  ON  NU  UN  NY  YN
PA  AP  PE  EP  PI  IP  PO  OP  PU  UP  PY  YP
QA  AQ  QE  EQ  QI  IQ  QO  OQ  QU  UQ  QY  YQ
RA  AR  RE  ER  RI  IR  RO  OR  RU  UR  RY  YR
SA  AS  SE  ES  SI  IS  SO  OS  SU  US  SY  YS
TA  AT  TE  ET  TI  IT  TO  OT  TU  UT  TY  YT
VA  AV  VE  EV  VI  IV  VO  OV  VU  UV  VY  YV
WA  AW  WE  EW  WI  IW  WO  OW  WU  UW  WY  YW
XA  AX  XE  EX  XI  IX  XO  OX  XU  UX  XY  YX
ZA  AZ  ZE  EZ  ZI  IZ  ZO  OZ  ZU  UZ  ZY  YZ
```

Further Notes on Program 27:

1. The PRINT statement that displays the output is executed 120 times in this program. The blanks are inserted to make the output readable.

2. The two loops that read in the vowels and consonants both use the index variable I, which is permissible because the loops are independent of one another. However, in the nested loop structure, the variable I and a second variable J must be used.

3. When the keyword PRINT appears by itself, it acts as a carriage return. Note how it is strategically placed between the two NEXT statements.

4. You may note that 26 of the 240 pairs of letters listed in the output are words in the English language.

C. THE BUBBLE SORT

To sort data is to put the data items into a specific order. Four possible sorting schemes are:

(1) character data in alphabetical order (A to Z),

(2) character data in reverse alphabetical order (Z to A),

(3) numerical data in increasing order,

(4) numerical data in decreasing order.

All of these sorts can be accomplished by a sorting algorithm known as the *bubble sort*. (Many sorting algorithms exist. The bubble sort is one of the easiest to understand and thus it is presented in this introduction to sorting.) The bubble sort compares two adjacent elements in an array, and if necessary, swaps their positions to fit a desired order. The sort relies entirely on the subscripts of the array elements to keep track of the comparisons. Before you develop the sorting algorithm, let us see how a swap can be accomplished. Suppose you want to interchange the values of X(1) and X(2). A naive (and incorrect) set of statements that you could try is

```
LET X(1) = X(2)
LET X(2) = X(1)
```

To see why these statements do not accomplish the swap, assume that the values 5 and 10 have been assigned to X(1) and X(2), respectively. Figure 4.4 shows the results of the above statements on X(1) and X(2).

	VALUE OF X(1)	VALUE OF X(2)
	5	10
LET X(1) = X(2)	10	10
LET X(2) = X(1)	10	10

Figure 4.4. An Attempt to Interchange the Values of X(1) and X(2)

The assignment statement X(1)=X(2) destroys the original value of X(1). What is needed is another copy of X(1) so that when the destructive assignment to X(1) occurs, the value 5 is still available. The general approach is to use another variable, say TEMP, as a temporary holding place for a copy of the value 5. In Figure 4.5 the values of X(1) and X(2) are traced as the standard three-statement sequence to swap two values is executed.

	VALUE OF		
	X(1)	X(2)	Temp
	5	10	0
LET TEMP = X(1)	5	10	5
LET X(1) = X(2)	10	10	5
LET X(2) = TEMP	10	5	5

Figure 4.5. Values of X(1) and X(2) Interchanged

To demonstrate the bubble sort, consider an array A with four cells containing the entries 20, 12, 8, and 2, in that order. Suppose that the numbers are to be sorted into increasing order, so that at the end of the sort, A(1) = 2, A(2) = 8, A(3) = 12, and A(4) = 20. Consider Figure 4.6, where PASS and PAIR are used to identify the various steps (and are later used in nested loops in the bubble sort program). Three sets of comparisons through the array are needed. The variable PASS corresponds to the set of comparisons currently being processed. The variable PAIR denotes the particular position PAIR in the array A. Referring to Figure 4.6, when PASS = 1 and PAIR = 1, A(1) = 20, and A(2) = 12 are compared (represented by the two-headed arrow) and interchanged because the values are to be in increasing order. When PASS = 1 and PAIR = 2, A(2), and A(3) are compared and in this case interchanged. Then when PASS = 1 and PAIR = 3, A(3) and A(4) are compared and also interchanged. Note that the maximum value of PAIR is 3. Thus the first pass through the array results in A(1) = 12, A(2) = 8, A(3) = 2, and A(4) = 20. Only the number 20 is in its correct final position at this point.

The second set of comparisons, corresponding to PASS = 2, is shown in the second row of Figure 4.6. Note that the comparison when PAIR = 3 is unnecessary because the values 12 and 20 are already in their final positions.

The final pass through the array sets up the last three comparisons. Note that only the first of these (PASS = 3, PAIR = 1) is needed. By the time PASS = 3 and PAIR = 2, the numbers are already in increasing order. As depicted in Figure 4.6, in a bubble sort the little numbers float up like bubbles to the top of the array.

Before the sorting program is presented, a measure will be considered to make the program as efficient as possible. Figure 4.6 shows nine comparisons, only six of which are really necessary. Earlier, it was mentioned that nested loops would be used in the bubble sort. However, the statements

```
FOR PASS = 1 TO 3
FOR PAIR = 1 TO 3
```

represent all nine comparisons. To delete the unnecessary comparisons, you can use the statements

```
FOR PASS = 1 TO 3
FOR PAIR = 1 TO 4-PASS
```

Note that when PASS = 1, the inner loop is executed when PAIR = 1, 2, and 3, which leads to three comparisons on the first pass. When PASS = 2, the inner loop is executed for PAIR = 1 and PAIR = 2, so that two comparisons are established during the second pass. Finally, when PASS = 3, PAIR = 1 only, leading to just the single necessary comparison A(1) to A(2) on the third pass through the array.

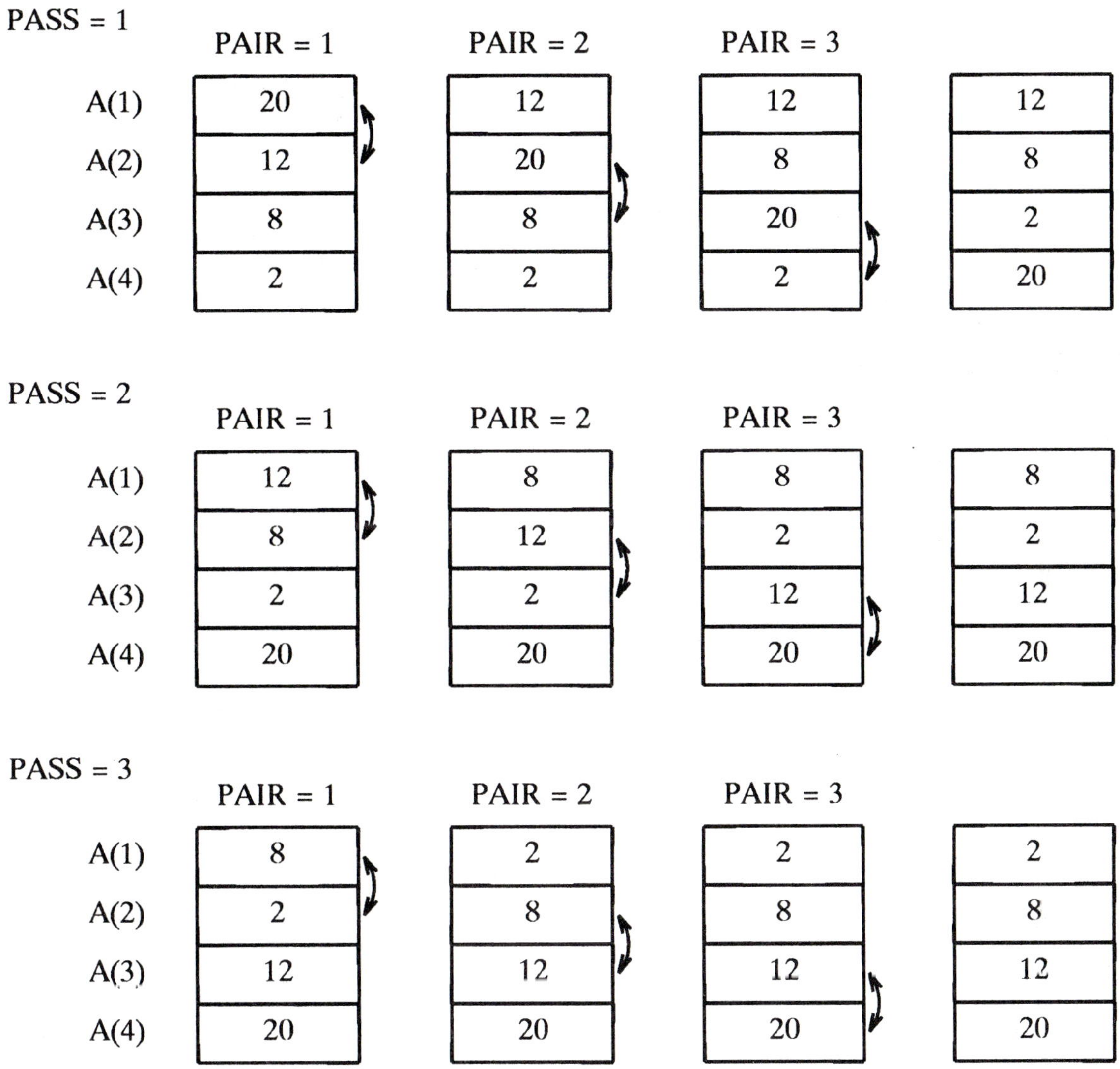

Figure 4.6. Bubble Sort Comparisons

Program 28 contains the bubble sort routine.

Program 28.

```
REM  BUBBLE SORT USING NESTED LOOPS,
REM  ASSUME ARRAY HAS 4 ELEMENTS
DIM A(4)
GOSUB INITIALIZE
FOR PASS = 1 TO 3
  FOR PAIR = 1 TO 4 - PASS
    IF A(PAIR) > A(PAIR + 1) THEN GOSUB SWAPPAIR
  NEXT PAIR
NEXT PASS
GOSUB PRINTOUT
END

REM ********** SUBROUTINE SECTION *******************
REM ******* SUBROUTINE TO FILL THE ARRAY *********
INITIALIZE:
FOR I = 1 TO 4
 READ A(I)
NEXT I
DATA 8, 20, 2, 12
RETURN

REM ** SUBROUTINE TO INTERCHANGE TWO VALUES **
SWAPPAIR:
LET TEMP = A(PAIR + 1)
LET A(PAIR + 1) = A(PAIR)
LET A(PAIR) = TEMP
RETURN

REM ***** SUBROUTINE TO PRINT THE ARRAY *********
PRINTOUT:
FOR I = 1 TO 4
 PRINT A(I)
NEXT I
RETURN
```

Output:

```
2
8
12
20
```

Further Notes on Program 28:

1. This program can be modified easily to sort an array of any size. You are encouraged to find the lines that would have to be modified.
2. If character string data were involved, you would need to replace all the references to the numeric arrays A and TEMP with string arrays A$ and TEMP$, respectively. When discussing character strings, A < B < C < ... < Z, so that to sort the entries of a string array into increasing order is to alphabetize those entries.
3. To sort the numerical entries of array A into decreasing order, only one small change in this program is necessary: change "< =" to "> =".
4. QuickBASIC also has a SWAP statement. However, we created our own swap routine to show you the logic required to interchange two values.

A problem that requires the sorting of two arrays simultaneously is given at the end of this chapter (see Programming Problem 3).

D. TWO-DIMENSIONAL ARRAYS

It turns out that Mom wasn't satisfied with the array she learned about in Section B of this chapter, as depicted in Figure 4.1. Using that array, at the end of the year she could display the sum of the rents for the entire year earned from each of the 20 rooms. However, she could not see a month-by-month display of the earnings from each room. What she really wanted is shown in Figure 4.7.

	Jan	Feb	Mar	Apr	May	Jun	Jul	Aug	Sept	Oct	Nov	Dec
1												
2												
3												
4												
5												
6												
7												
8												
9												
10												
11												
12												
13												
14												
15												
16												
17												
18												
19												
20												

Figure 4.7. Mom's Two-Dimensional Display

Upon consulting one of her renters, she found that all she needed was a two-dimensional array, one that conceptually to the programmer has rows and columns. The 20 rows could represent the rooms 1, 2, 3, ... 20 and the 12 columns could represent the 12 months of the year. The resulting array would have 240 cells and could be dimensioned in a program through the use of the DIM statement

```
DIM R(20, 12)
```

Note that the number of rows is listed first, then the number of columns.

The individual cells in R are identified by two subscripts. For example, the cell containing the January rent for room 3 is denoted by R(3,1), whereas the March rent for room 1 is the contents of R(1,3).

Two-dimensional (also called rectangular) arrays are useful when depicting the relationship between two quantities that vary. In Mom's case, the room numbers and the months of the year vary. Although such two-dimensional displays are helpful to the programmer, in main memory these 240 cells are still in a linear order. The double subscript is just another way to name these storage locations. In fact, another common name for a two-dimensional array is a "double-subscripted" array.

How is data assigned to cells in a two-dimensional array and how is this data printed out? As you might guess, because there are two subscripts involved, nested FOR/NEXT loops will be implemented. For example, the following program segment would fill the array N with five rows and three columns.

```
DIM N(5,3)
FOR I = 1 TO 5
  FOR J = 1 TO 3
    READ N(I,J)
  NEXT J
NEXT I
DATA 10, 20, 30, 40, 50, 60, 70, 80, 90
DATA 100, 110, 120, 130, 140, 150
```

Note that with the above code, N is filled row-by-row; i.e., the cells are assigned values in the following sequence: N(1,1), N(1,2), N(1,3), N(2,1), etc. Another nested loop construction would print out the 15 values:

```
FOR I = 1 TO 5
  FOR J = 1 TO 3
    PRINT N(I,J)
  NEXT J
NEXT I
```

Using this code the output would appear as 15 numbers in one column. If you wanted a row and column output to correspond to the conceptually rectangular, five-row and three-column array, then the following code would be used:

```
FOR I = 1 TO 5
  FOR J = 1 TO 3
    PRINT N(I,J);
  NEXT J
  PRINT
NEXT I
```

Getting back to Mom's application and her array R with 20 rows and 12 columns, how could Mom determine the year's total income from, say, room 15? Obviously, she would add the rent received each month for that room. This corresponds to adding the entries in the fifteenth row of array R. The following program would allow Mom to add the entries in any row.

Program 29.

```
REM  PROGRAM TO TOTAL A ROW OF ARRAY R
DIM R(20, 12)
FOR I = 1 TO 20
  FOR J = 1 TO 12
    READ R(I, J)
  NEXT J
NEXT I
LET TOTAL = 0
PRINT "WHICH ROW DO YOU WANT ADDED?"
INPUT ROW
FOR J = 1 TO 12
  LET TOTAL = TOTAL + R(ROW, J)
NEXT J
PRINT "SUM OF ROW"; ROW; "IS"; TOTAL
DATA (240 entries)
END
```

Further Notes on Program 29:

1. The TOTAL calculated in this program is the sum R(ROW,1) + R(ROW,2) + ... + R(ROW,12).
2. Because of the way the nested loops are written, the data in the DATA statements must be entered in a specific order, namely row by row. In other words, all of the monthly rental amounts for room 1 are entered, then the amounts for room 2, and so on.

If Mom needed to know the total income for any given month, she would merely add the rent received for that month for each of the 20 rooms. This corresponds to adding the entries in a specific column of array R. The following changes to Program 29 would allow her to add the entries in any column.

```
PRINT "WHICH COLUMN DO YOU WANT ADDED?"
INPUT COLUMN
FOR I = 1 TO 20
   LET TOTAL = TOTAL + R(I,COLUMN)
NEXT I
PRINT "SUM OF COLUMN"; COLUMN; "IS"; TOTAL
```

Finally if Mom wants to know the rental income for the entire year, she would simply add all the entries in the array R. The following program calculates this sum row by row.

Program 30.

```
REM  PROGRAM TO TOTAL ALL ELEMENTS IN R.
DIM R(20,12)
LET TOTAL = 0
FOR I = 1 TO 20
  FOR J = 1 TO 12
    READ R(I,J)
    LET TOTAL = TOTAL + R(I,J)
  NEXT J
NEXT I
PRINT "THE SUM IS"; TOTAL
DATA (240 entries)
END
```

The flowchart for Program 30 is given in Figure 4.8. Note how the dimensioning of the array and the nesting of loops is depicted.

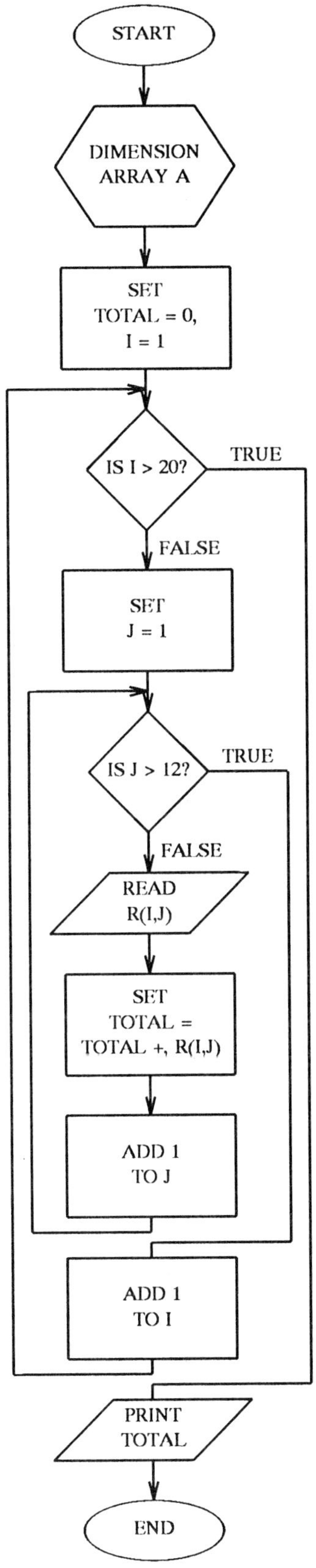

Figure 4.8. Flowchart for Program 30

E. REVIEW EXERCISES

1. Write a QuickBASIC statement or program segment that
   (a) defines an array A containing 40 numeric elements,
   (b) reads 40 numbers into the array A,
   (c) swaps elements 20 and 30 in array A.

2. What will happen when the following program is run?

```
DIM M(5)
FOR I = 1 TO 5
  READ M(I)
  PRINT M(I)
NEXT I
DATA 4, 3, 2, 1
END
```

3. Show the output of the following program segment.

```
DIM N$(2,3)
FOR I = 1 TO 2
  FOR J = 1 TO 3
    READ N$(I,J)
  NEXT J
NEXT I
FOR K = 1 TO 2
  PRINT N$(K,2)
NEXT K
DATA JOE, SAM, SUE, ROY, KIM, KAY
```

4. Determine the value of S after each of the following program segments has been executed. The contents of N(1) to N(8) are:

(1)	(2)	(3)	(4)	(5)	(6)	(7)	(8)
4	8	0	2	2	1	3	1

(a)
```
S = N(1) - N(7) + 1
```

(b)
```
S = 0
FOR I = 4 TO 8
  S = S + N(I)
NEXT I
```

(c) N(1) = N(8)
N(2) = N(4)
S = N(1) + N(2)

(d) I = N(6)
S = N(I) - I

5. Change the appropriate lines in Program 30 so that the sum of all of the elements in array R is found column by column.

6. If the two arrays used in Program 27 each held all 26 letters of the alphabet, how many pairs of letters would be printed in the output? How many *new* two-letter English words would be printed using these larger arrays?

7. Modify Program 26 so that all matches between the entries in the array FIRST and those in SECOND are printed. In other words, if the number 7 appears once in FIRST and three times in SECOND, it should be printed three times.

8. Modify Program 26 to eliminate the printing of duplicates in the array FIRST. In other words, if the number 27 appears twice in the array FIRST and is also in the array SECOND, then it should only appear once in the printed output. (This problem is considerably harder than the previous one.)

9. Suppose a numerical array A with 20 entries (but with room for more than 20 entries) has been sorted, with numbers in increasing order. Write a *program segment* to insert a new entry into the array so that after completing the process, the array is once again in increasing order.

F. LAB EXERCISE

An array is a collection of variables. If you have a list of names or scores, for example, you can refer to the collection of names or scores by using arrays. If you have 20 scores, you can use an array named SCORE with 20 "storage cells" to hold the scores. The first score would be put into SCORE(1), pronounced SCORE sub one, the second score would be put into SCORE(2), the third score would be put into SCORE(3), and so on until the last score (i.e., the twetieth) would be put into SCORE(20).

To begin this exercise, type in the following program that assigns values to the 20 elements of the array SCORE. Use any numbers you wish for the input statements.

```
DIM SCORE(20)
PRINT "TYPE IN TWENTY SCORES"
INPUT SCORE(1)
INPUT SCORE(2)
INPUT SCORE(3)
INPUT SCORE(4)
INPUT SCORE(5)
```

```
INPUT SCORE(6)
INPUT SCORE(7)
INPUT SCORE(8)
INPUT SCORE(9)
INPUT SCORE(10)
INPUT SCORE(11)
INPUT SCORE(12)
INPUT SCORE(13)
INPUT SCORE(14)
INPUT SCORE(15)
INPUT SCORE(16)
INPUT SCORE(17)
INPUT SCORE(18)
INPUT SCORE(19)
INPUT SCORE(20)
END
```

The DIM statement tells the computer that you are using an array with a specific name and a specific number of cells. So if you needed another array in this program to hold the class (we'll denote the class of freshmen, sophomores, juniors, and seniors by the numbers 1, 2, 3, and 4, respectively) of the student obtaining each score, this declaration would be given as

DIM CLASS(20)

What if you wanted to count the number of students in each class? You could use an array with four cells (one for each class) and call it COUNT. Write the statement to establish this array.

____

So far, you have merely assigned values to the cells of the array SCORE through the input statements. Obviously, using 20 INPUT statements is not a very efficient way to fill an array. There has to be a better approach! If you look closely at the number inside the parentheses (the subscript), you'll note that it is the only thing that changes in the 20 INPUT statements. It increases from 1 to 2 to 3, etc. In other words, you can store a number in SCORE(I) and the next number in SCORE(I+1), etc. Note that you are just counting with an increment of 1, and you already have a pair of statements in BASIC that helps you do this. If you haven't already quessed what these statements are, here is a hint. Clear out your computer's main memory, and then enter and execute this small program.

```
FOR I = 1 TO 20
  PRINT I
NEXT I
END
```

Notice that the variable I changes from 1 to 2 to 3 to 4, all the way up to 20. Doesn't the subscript do the same in the above program? There must be way to combine loops and arrays to make entering values easier. Clear memory again, and then enter and execute the following program. Enter any values you wish at the prompt.

```
DIM SCORE(20)
FOR I = 1 TO 20
  INPUT SCORE(I)
NEXT I
END
```

When I = 1, where is the number stored?

____

When I = 10, where is the number stored?

____

This approach to entering scores into an array is easy. You have used the control variable from the FOR/NEXT loop as the array subscript. Referencing array elements is a common and important use of the FOR/NEXT loop.

Remember, an array variable is just a variable – you put data of some kind in it. You always refer to it by name and subscript. If you just asked for SCORE, you would not be requesting the value of any of the 20 cells in the array. (SCORE would just be some other simple, non-array variable.)

Now you can print out the scores we assigned to the array. Remember, there are 20 of them, but instead of using 20 print statements, you can again use a FOR/NEXT loop to print out the values. Modify your program to include

```
FOR I = 1 TO 20
   PRINT SCORE(I)
NEXT I
```

Run your program.

What if you changed the control variable of the loop (the I) to J? What would happen and why?

____

____

Now you can do some calculations with the scores. Add the following to your program:

```
REM FINDING THE AVERAGE OF THE SCORES
TOTAL = 0
FOR I = 1 TO 20
  TOTAL = TOTAL + SCORE(I)
NEXT I
PRINT "THE AVERAGE IS ";TOTAL/20
```

Run your program.

Look at the listing for your program. You will see that you have three FOR/NEXT loops. Can you replace those three loops with one loop? Can you input, print, and find a total all in one loop? If so, write the loop below.

Add the CLASS information to your program.

(a) Add the declaration for the array CLASS and COUNT.
(b) Include in the input statement the variable CLASS for holding the class type.
(c) Include in the print statement the variable for printing out the class type.
(d) Add a loop to zero out all the elements in the array called COUNT.
(e) After the statement that accumulates the scores include the following:

```
COUNT(CLASS(I)) = COUNT(CLASS(I)) + 1
```

Note that the contents of CLASS(I) is one of the values 1, 2, 3, or 4. Thus when CLASS(I) equals 1, you are incrementing COUNT(1), the variable that holds the total number of freshmen, by 1. You obtain similar results when CLASS(I) equals 2, 3, or 4.

(f) Add a loop to print out the number of scores in each class. Run this final version of your program.

G. PROGRAMMING PROBLEMS

1. Write a BASIC program that simulates the rolling of two dice. The program should use the random number generator to "roll" each die and then calculate and print the sum of the two values. Because each die can show a value of 1 to 6, the sum can vary from 2 to 12. Use a single-subscripted array N to tally the number of times each possible sum appears, much like the way the responses to the poll were tallied in Program 25. The program should throw the two dice 100 times and print out the number of times each sum appears.

2. Write a BASIC program that will accept up to 100 names as input (either through an INPUT or a READ statement), sort the names, and output a list of the names in correct alphabetical order. Demonstrate the effectiveness of your program by entering the names

of 10 of your friends. Output should take the form of an alphabetized list with one name per line, last name first. Skip one line between each name. Precede the list with an appropriate heading. A FOR/NEXT loop should be used to control input so that the user can specify exactly how many names to enter. Use the bubble sort technique for alphabetizing the names.

3. Assume that the data listed below are names and test scores from a computer science class. Write a BASIC program that will give the user a menu that can be used to

   (1) output the names and corresponding test scores, where the names are in alphabetical order,

   (2) output the names and corresponding test scores, where the scores are listed in decreasing order,

   (3) exit from the program.

   Your program should allow the user to choose an option from the menu by means of a SELECT CASE statement as many times as the user wishes. The output should be one name (last name first) and score per line. Also skip one line between each line of output and precede each listing with an appropriate heading. To facilitate sorting, put the names into a character string array and the numbers into a numerical array. Use the bubble sort technique for both sorts.

   The data to be used (entered in this order) in this program are as follows:

Thomas, Gerald	94
Allen, Mark	81
Stevens, Mary	68
Connors, Debbie	100
Ellis, Ruth	75
Johnson, Robert	68
Lane, Felix	97
Wilson, David	98
Rasmic, Linda	83
Breiner, Joe	55
McBride, Karen	80
Nelson, Charles	70

4. Program 29 enabled Mom to add any row of the array R. Modifications then were given so that any column could be added. Finally, Program 30 enabled Mom to add all 240 entries in R. It would seem reasonable to combine these three options into one program. Write a BASIC program using a smaller array N with 10 rows and 5 columns that will give the user a menu that can be used to

   (1) add any row in N,

   (2) add any column in N,

   (3) add all of the entries in N,

   (4) exit the program.

   Your program should allow the user to choose an option from the menu by means of a SELECT CASE statement as many times as desired. Each time a sum is found, use a

PRINT statement to describe the sum and print the total.

5. Mom is playing "movable renters" today. The rooms 1, 2, 3 ... 18 are rented and rooms 19 and 20 are vacant. Two of her own children decide to visit for the summer, but they plead with Mom to let them stay in their old rooms, numbered 1 and 2. Mom has decided to accommodate her newcomers and she has asked all of her renters to simply move down two rooms. They have all agreed to pay the same rent as they paid before the move. (Apparently they believe the rent would normally increase as the room number increased.) The problem of course is the record keeping. Mom had non-zero rents coming from rooms 1 through 18. The contents of these cells in the array R are to be moved two cells to the locations 3 through 20, respectively. Because Mom will not charge her own offspring rent, the new values of R(1) and R(2) in the array are to be zero.

   Write a program segment for Mom that will manipulate elements in the array R as described and set R(1) = R(2) = 0.

   (*Hint*: Use a FOR/NEXT loop with a negative increment.)

6. Write a QuickBASIC program that will read the following set of test data into a double-subscripted array.

Student No.	Test #1	Test #2	Test #3	Test #4
1	90	80	70	60
2	85	75	65	95
3	72	44	53	65
4	55	66	77	88
5	99	99	99	99
6	84	85	86	88
7	74	75	73	70
8	40	45	33	67
9	86	83	90	91
10	100	87	86	88
11	69	74	78	73
12	88	84	81	90

   The program should allow the user the options described below.

   OPTION #1: The user is asked if a particular student's test average is wanted. If the answer is "no", the computer moves on to Option #2. If the answer is "yes", the user supplies the student number and the computer provides each score for that student and gives the test average as well.

OPTION #2: The user is asked if the class average for a particular test is wanted. If the answer is "no", the computer moves on to Option #3. If the answer is "yes", the user indicates which test, and the computer provides a list of all scores for that test and then gives the class average.

OPTION #3: The computer asks the user if a list of the individual averages for all students is wanted. On a "no" response, the computer moves to Option #4. A "yes" response results in the output of a table of all student scores along with the individual averages.

OPTION #4: Here the user is asked if the class averages for all tests is wanted. A "no" response causes the computer to ask if the user is ready to end the program; if "yes" the program terminates, if "no" the computer returns to Option #1. A "yes" response to the original question here causes the computer to print a table of all test scores along with the class average for each test.

You should carefully organize the messages to the user, as well as the general formatting of output. The test scores are to be entered through the READ/DATA method of input, but the balance of the program is to be interactive in nature.

7. Your product department has just invented a new product, the Whirly Disk. It requires five parts in the manufacturing process, and these parts are distributed in four warehouses across the country. Listed below by number are the five parts, their cost, and the number of each part currently in each warehouse.

Part #	Cost	Warehouse			
		1	2	3	4
1	.67	600	332	241	1000
2	.99	800	92	505	400
3	1.10	225	432	392	125
4	4.00	88	99	362	428
5	.25	85	89	125	320

You are asked by the inventory department to write a program that aids in controlling inventory. They have identified the following 10 tasks that are to be incorporated into your program. Your program should provide

(1) a printout of the inventory of parts for Whirly Disks (as shown in the table above),

(2) a listing of the total number of units available for each part,

(3) a listing of the total dollars tied up in inventory for each part,

(4) a listing of the total dollars tied up in inventory for each part at each of the warehouses,

(5) a listing of the warehouse that holds the largest number of parts of each type, along with that largest value,

(6) a printout of the part type that has the least number of units available across the country,

(7) a listing of which parts have less than 1000 units available across the country, along with the total inventory for those parts,

(8) a listing of any part and warehouse when the number of units of that part falls below 50 at that particular warehouse,

(9) the capability to update (add and delete parts) the inventory report,

(10) a way to exit the program.

Your program should allow the user to choose an option from a menu as many times as desired. Use a double-subscripted array to hold your data.

8. Write a tic-tac-toe program that allows the user to enter successive moves and stops when either one player wins or all of the squares are filled. The following is an example of what the players should see:

```
WELCOME TO TIC-TAC-TOE
X MOVES NEXT
ENTER THE ROW AND COLUMN FOR MOVE 1
  1, 3

            |    | X
        ----+----+----
            |    |
        ----+----+----
            |    |

O MOVES NEXT
ENTER THE ROW AND COLUMN FOR MOVE 2
  2, 1

            |    | X
        ----+----+----
          O |    |
        ----+----+----
            |    |
```

Record all moves, each time incrementing the number of moves, checking for legal moves (no previous X or O in that position, row and column designations 1, 2, or 3, etc.), displaying the move and checking for a winner or end-of-game situation.

9. An investor's stock portfolio is listed below:

Name of Stock	Number of Shares	Current Week's Closing Price
Sterling Drug	800	$16.25
Data General	650	57.50
Owen Illinois	1200	21.50
Mattell, Inc.	1000	11.125
Abbott Lab	2000	34.75
Fed Natl. Mtg	2500	17.75
IC Gen	250	43.625
ALO Systems	550	18.25

Read the columns of the table into a program either as separate arrays or as a character array for the stock names and a two-dimensional real array for the number of shares and closing prices. Calculate the EQUITY (EQUITY = No. of Shares * Price) for each stock and store these values in an array. Use at least one DATA statement in your program. Your program should produce the following two reports:

Report 1: A four-column report including the above information and the EQUITY values. Include a TOTAL WORTH summary line.

Report 2: Sort the EQUITY values into descending order. Write a report indicating the stocks held and the value of the holdings (i.e., a two-column report in descending order of EQUITY). Remember, a swap in the equity column also means a swap in the stock identification column.

CHAPTER FIVE

CHARACTER STRING FUNCTIONS

"Suit the action to the word, the word to the action..." (William Shakespeare, 1564–1616, *Hamlet*, Act III, Scene 2.)

A. INTRODUCTION

In Chapters One through Four, we have concentrated on QuickBASIC programs using numeric data and numeric functions. Character strings have been used rather sparingly, appearing primarily as text to be printed through a PRINT statement or as data simply entered into a variable or an array. However, many fascinating applications that occur in personal and business-related areas require manipulating string data by using character string functions. Such functions give a programmer the power to join strings together, to search for specific characters or specific strings in character data, to extract parts of strings, and to determine the length of a string for further string manipulation.

By way of review, recall that a *character string* is a sequence of letters, numbers, or special characters enclosed in quotation marks. A character string variable in QuickBASIC must end in a dollar sign. The assignment of strings to string variables can, of course, be accomplished through a LET statement, an INPUT statement, or through the READ/DATA combination of statements. Examples showing these alternatives follow:

1. The output of the following code is the message TODAY IS MONDAY.

```
LET DAY$ = "MONDAY"
.
.
.
PRINT "TODAY IS "; DAY$
```

Note that a blank space follows the word IS. Without that space, the output would be TODAY ISMONDAY.

2. The following program segment allows the user to enter a character string to determine if a program should continue.

```
PRINT "SHALL WE CONTINUE?"
INPUT RESPONSE$
IF RESPONSE$ = "YES" GOSUB GAME
PRINT "THANK YOU FOR PLAYING."
END
```

Note that any input other than "YES" (e.g., "yes" or "Y") would not allow the user to continue playing.

3. The READ/DATA statements are still appropriate with character string data when a large amount of data needs to be entered into a program. A short example is:

```
READ LOCATION1$, LOCATION2$
  .
  .
  .
DATA "CHICAGO, ILLINOIS"
DATA "MUNCIE, INDIANA"
```

You will see programs using these three data entry methods in the examples that follow.

B. COMPARING MATHEMATICAL AND CHARACTER STRING FUNCTIONS

Mathematical built-in functions, including INT(X), RND, and SQR(X) were presented in Chapter Three. These functions have numeric operands and always return a numeric value. In this chapter, the built-in character string functions are discussed. These functions can have string and numeric operands and can return a character string or a numeric value. Examples of such functions and a summary of these remarks appear in Table 5.1.

FUNCTION TYPE	OPERANDS	RETURNS	EXAMPLES
Mathematical	Numbers	A Number	SQR INT ABS
String	Strings and/or Numbers	A String or a Number	LEN LEFT$ INSTR

Table 5.1. Comparing Mathematical and String Functions

C. COMMON STRING FUNCTIONS

The operation of concatenation and the common character string functions that are used in the examples and exercises of this chapter are presented in this section. You are encouraged to consult a user's manual for a complete list of such functions available on any particular system.

1. *CONCATENATION.* To concatenate strings is to connect two or more strings using the + sign.

   For example, the execution of the statements

   ```
   A$ = "JACK"
   B$ = "FROST"
   C$ = A$ + B$
   PRINT C$
   ```

   results in the printing of the string JACKFROST. If a space is desired between K and F in the above example, you could use A$ = "JACK " or B$ = " FROST" or C$ = A$ + " " + B$. Although the "+" sign looks the same as the one used for the arithmetic operation of addition, QuickBASIC knows that concatenation is the intended operation here.

2. *LEN*(A$). The length function LEN gives the number of characters in A$, and thus LEN always returns an integer value.

   The execution of the following code would result in the printing of the number 16.

   ```
   A$ = "COMPUTER SCIENCE"
   PRINT LEN(A$)
   ```

3. *LEFT$*(A$, N). This function obtains a portion of A$, N characters long, starting at the leftmost position of A$. N may be an integer expression or a constant.

   The following statements would result in the printing of the string JACK.

   ```
   A$ = "JACK FROST"
   PRINT LEFT$(A$,4)
   ```

4. *RIGHT$*(A$, N). This function obtains a portion of A$ consisting of the rightmost N characters of A$. N may be an integer expression or a constant. (The definition of this function varies in different versions of BASIC.) The next example would print ROST.

   ```
   A$ = "JACK FROST"
   PRINT RIGHT$(A$,4)
   ```

5. *MID$*(A$, N1, N2). The midstring function MID$ obtains a portion of A$, N2 characters long beginning at position N1 in the middle of the string.

The string THE would be printed after the following lines are executed. Note that a blank counts because it is a legal character.

```
A$ = ''JACK THE FROST''
PRINT MID$(A$,6,3)
```

Note that N1 and N2 may be integer expressions or constants. Note also that N2 is the *length* of the string, and not the ending position.

6. *INSTR*(N, A$, B$). This function searches A$ starting at position N to determine where a substring B$ begins in A$. (INSTR returns an integer value.) If B$ does not appear in A$, this function returns a value of zero. Again, N may be an integer expression or a constant.

The output of the following five statements are the numbers 6, 0, 6, 6, and 0, respectively.

```
PRINT INSTR(1, ''BLACKSMITH'', ''S'')
PRINT INSTR(1, ''BLACKSMITH'', ''R'')
PRINT INSTR(1, ''BLACKSMITH'', ''SMITH'')
PRINT INSTR(3, ''BLACKSMITH'', ''S'')
PRINT INSTR(3, ''BLACKSMITH'', ''B'')
```

7. *SPACE$*(N). This function provides a string of N blanks where N is an integer expression or a constant. The SPACE$ function is useful when creating precise headings, as in the next statement.

```
PRINT ''YEAR''; SPACE$(5); ''INTEREST''; SPACE$(5); ''VALUE''
```

It results in the following output, where the underscores (_) represent blanks:

```
YEAR_____INTEREST_____VALUE
```

8. *ASC*(A$). This function, usually written as ASC(A$), returns the numerical value that is the ASCII code of the first character of the string A$. The ASCII code for the uppercase letters A, B, C, ... Z are the numbers 65, 66, 67, ...90, respectively. For example, the execution of the statements

```
A$ = ''BASIC''
PRINT ASC(A$)
```

results in the printing of the value 66.

9. *CHR$(n)*. The character string function, CHR$, returns the one character string with ASCII code *n* (*n* must be in the range 0 to 255). CHR$ can be used to send a special character to the screen or printer that can result in such features as a line feed, a carriage return, or a beep. (Consult your user's manual for details.) The statement

```
PRINT CHR$(66)
```

results in the output of a "B".

Note that when a character string function's name ends in a $ (as in LEFT$, RIGHT$, MID$, SPACE$, and CHR$) the function returns a character string. Otherwise, (as in LEN, INSTR, and ASC), the function returns a numeric value. More examples showing the power and versatility of these functions follow.

Program 31.

Step 1. Describe the problem.

Just for the fun of it, let's write a program that takes a name entered in the form JOHN SMITH and puts it in the form SMITH, JOHN. (This could be useful as a program segment in a larger program, where names have been entered in the order first name, last name and a list alphabetized by last name is required.) For the purpose of this short program, assume the names will be entered from the terminal and only a first name and a last name will be entered. Output will be the first and last names reversed.

Step 2. Design the logic of the solution.

Let the name be entered into the variable FULLNAME$. Then the key to reverse the names is to find the blank between the first and last name. The search for the blank can be accomplished with a FOR/NEXT loop, searching through FULLNAME$ one character at a time using the MID$ function. Suppose the blank occurs in position I of FULLNAME$. Then the characters to the left of position I represent the first name and those to the right of the Ith position comprise the last name. The first and last name can be isolated by using the LEFT$ and RIGHT$ functions, respectively, and then printed in the required order.

Step 3. Code the program.

Two versions of this program are presented. In the first version, concatenation and the four string functions LEN, MID$, LEFT$, and RIGHT$ are used. The second version uses the powerful INSTR function to replace MID$ and the FOR/NEXT loop found in the first version.

FIRST VERSION:

```
REM  PROGRAM TO REVERSE FIRST AND LAST NAMES
INPUT "ENTER NAME"; FULLNAME$
LET I = 1

REM **** LOOKING FOR THE FIRST BLANK ********
I = 1
WHILE MID$(FULLNAME$, I, 1) <> " " AND I <= LEN(FULLNAME$)
   I = I + 1
WEND

REM **** DETERMINE IF A BLANK WAS FOUND ****
IF I > LEN(FULLNAME$) THEN
   PRINT "THERE WAS NO BLANK IN THE NAME."
ELSE
   FIRST$ = LEFT$(FULLNAME$, I - 1)
   LAST$ = RIGHT$(FULLNAME$, LEN(FULLNAME$) - I)
   PRINT LAST$ + ", " + FIRST$
END IF
END
```

SECOND VERSION:

```
REM PROGRAM TO REVERSE FIRST AND LAST NAMES
INPUT "ENTER NAME"; FULLNAME$
K = INSTR(1,FULLNAME$," ")
IF K = 0 THEN
   PRINT "NO BLANK IN NAME"
ELSE
   FIRST$ = LEFT$(FULLNAME$, K - 1)
   LAST$ = RIGHT$(FULLNAME$, LEN(FULLNAME$) - K)
   PRINT LAST$ + ", " + FIRST$
END IF
END
```

Further Notes on Program 31:

1. You should study how the situation where no blank appears in the name has been addressed in each of the versions of this program.
2. No provision is made for middle names or middle initials in this program. If two blanks occur, as in the name JOHN FRANK WILSON, the program just considers the second blank as another character in the last name.
3. The printing of the name reversed could be accomplished without concatenation by using the statement

```
PRINT LAST$; ", "; FIRST$
```

Program 32.

Step 1. Describe the problem.

You want to write a program to detect palindromes. (A *palindrome* is a character string that is the same when read forward or backward. Examples of palindromes include the words *mom, dad, level, racecar* and *radar*, and, after you delete the spaces, the string "a man a plan a canal panama".) The string will be entered at the terminal. The output should be the string and a message as to whether or not it is a palindrome.

Step 2. Design the logic of the solution.

Let FORWARD$ contain the entered character string. Then append in reverse order the individual characters of FORWARD$ to another variable, say BACKWARD$. To accomplish this, BACKWARD$ will be initialized to the null string "" (analogous to initializing a summing numerical variable to 0) and concatenation will be used to append letters to BACKWARD$. Concatenation must start with the last character of FORWARD$ and proceed to the first character of FORWARD$. Use a FOR/NEXT loop with a negative increment, and within it use MID$ to pick off the appropriate letters of FORWARD$, one at a time.

Step 3. Code the program.

```
REM  PROGRAM TO DETECT PALINDROMES.
PRINT "ENTER A CHARACTER STRING"
INPUT FORWARD$
LET BACKWARD$ = ""
REM  USING CONCATENATION TO APPEND, IN REVERSE ORDER,
REM  THE CHARACTERS OF FORWARD$ TO BACKWARD$.
FOR I = LEN(FORWARD$) TO 1 STEP -1
   LET BACKWARD$ = BACKWARD$ + MID$(FORWARD$, I, 1)
NEXT I
IF FORWARD$ = BACKWARD$ THEN
   PRINT FORWARD$;" IS A PALINDROME"
ELSE
   PRINT FORWARD$;" IS NOT A PALINDROME."
END IF
END
```

Program 33.

Step 1. Describe the problem.

You want to write a program to determine how many words in a given list contain a specific sequence of letters – for example, *MENT*. You will READ the words into the program from DATA lines. The output should consist of an appropriate heading and a list of those words containing *MENT*.

Step 2. Design the logic of the solution.

First, READ the words into the variable WORD$. Then you can use a WHILE/WEND loop with index J to search each word for the four-letter sequence *MENT* by means of the MID$ function. You will continue searching for *MENT* while J is less than or equal to LEN(WORD$)-3 because there is no need to continue searching for *MENT* if there are less than four letters to check. If *MENT* is contained in the word, that word is printed. This entire process is to be done for each word in the list of words. Therefore, the previously mentioned loop will be contained in a FOR/NEXT loop with index I whose limit value is equal to the number of words in the list. (This example will process 10 words.)

Step 3. Code the program.

```
REM  PROGRAM TO PRINT WORDS CONTAINING THE
REM  4-LETTER SEQUENCE MENT
PRINT "WORDS CONTAINING MENT"
PRINT
FOR I = 1 TO 10
   READ WORD$
   J = 1
   WHILE J <= LEN(WORD$)-3
      IF MID$(WORD$,J,4) = "MENT" THEN PRINT WORD$
      J = J + 1
  WEND
NEXT I
DATA COMPUTING, AUGMENTING
DATA TESTAMENT, ANALYSIS, PARLIAMENTARY
DATA PREDICAMENT, MENTOR
DATA FLING, CREDITOR, PERMANENT
END
```

Output:

```
WORDS CONTAINING MENT

AUGMENTING
TESTAMENT
PARLIAMENTARY
PREDICAMENT
MENTOR
```

Further Notes on Program 33:

1. If the sequence to be found contained only three letters, such as ING, then the WHILE and IF statements would be changed as follows:

```
WHILE J < = LEN(WORD$)-2
 IF MID$(WORD$,J,3) = ''ING'' THEN PRINT WORD$
```

2. If the number of words in the list was not known, a character string trailer could be used to end the program. A WHILE statement could be used to check for the trailer. The WHILE/WEND loop would then replace the FOR/NEXT loop that is used here. (Recall that a similar procedure was used in Programs 7 and 14.)

Program 34.

Step1. Describe the problem.

The FBI (Fun Bunch of Investigators) has just discovered a dissident group of outrageous teenage mutant rabbits that have been sending secret messages through their underground bunny tunnels. You need to help the FBI by writing a decoder to unscramble the group's messages. Several messages have been intercepted, and it has been determined that the bunnies have been using a simple method, called a *shifting cipher*, to encode their messages. This cipher takes a letter and shifts it by a prescribed number of positions in the alphabet to a new letter. For example, the word *DOG* could be encoded in a secret message as ALD. Then if you know that the shift factor is 3, you can decode this message to recover the word *DOG*. Note that the shift ''wraps around'' the alphabet, so that a Y is mapped to a B with a three-letter shift.

Step 2. Design the logic of the solution.

The input to the program is the secret message and the shift factor, SHIFT. You'll allow SHIFT to change because you expect these brainy bunnies to vary their approach to sending messages. Because the shifting has a mathematical basis, you'll need to change characters to their ASCII code, perform the necessary calculations, and then change back to characters again using the CHR$ function. (You can assume the use of only uppercase characters, with ASCII representations 65 to 90.) Normal SHIFT values are in the range 1 to 26 because there are 26 letters in the alphabet. Your program will be able to handle shifts greater than 26 (if those rascally rabbits try to trick you) by means of arithmetic modulo 26. You simply divide the shift factor by 26 and get a remainder that then becomes the value of SHIFT. For example, if the shift factor entered is 29, dividing 29 by 26 gives a remainder of 3, which says that SHIFT equals 3. (This is reasonable if you consider that a shift of 29 positions means going through the entire alphabet once, plus three more positions.) You'll need to use MID$ to decode one character of the message at a time and LEN to determine the number of characters in the message.

Step 3. Code the program.

```
REM TEENAGE MUTANT RABBIT DECODER PROGRAM
REM A FORWARD SHIFTING CIPHER
PRINT "ENTER THE SECRET CODE IN UPPERCASE LETTERS."
INPUT MESSAGE$
PRINT "ENTER THE SHIFT IN THE ALPHABET."
INPUT SHIFT
IF SHIFT > 26 THEN SHIFT = SHIFT - INT(SHIFT/26) * 26
FOR I = 1 TO LEN(MESSAGE$)
  LETTER$ = MID$(MESSAGE$, I, 1)
  IF LETTER$ = " " THEN
     PRINT " ";
  ELSE
     INDEX = ASC(LETTER$)
     IF INDEX + SHIFT > 90 THEN
        PRINT CHR$(INDEX + SHIFT - 26);
     ELSE
        PRINT CHR$(INDEX + SHIFT);
     END IF
  END IF
NEXT I
PRINT
END
```

Sample Output:

```
ENTER THE SECRET CODE IN UPPERCASE LETTERS.
?ZXOOLQP XOB DOBXQ
ENTER THE SHIFT IN THE ALPHABET.
? 3
CARROTS ARE GREAT
```

Sample Output:

```
ENTER THE SECRET CODE IN UPPERCASE LETTERS.
?CARROTS ARE GREAT
ENTER THE SHIFT IN THE ALPHABET.
? 23
ZXOOLQP XOB DOBXQ
```

Further Notes on Program 34:

1. Note that you have actually nested one IF...THEN...ELSE structure inside another in this program. QuickBASIC allows the nesting of selection structures as well as looping structures.

2. If INDEX + SHIFT <= 90, then there exists an uppercase letter represented by that ASCII value. However, if INDEX + SHIFT > 90, then an adjustment is made in that line to arrive at the correct character. Why is the subtraction of 26 in that line sufficient?

3. The second execution of this program shows that this "decoder" can also be used to "encode" a message. Note that the shift factor to encode is found by taking 26 minus the shift factor to decode. Why does this work?

D. REVIEW EXERCISES

1. Write a single QuickBASIC statement to perform each of the following:
   (a) Print the message "string is too long" if the variable N is less than the number of characters in the string A$.
   (b) Place in the variable C$ the first 8 characters of the concatenation of the string variables A$ and B$.
   (c) Print the first five characters of A$ if the 6th character of A$ is equal to "*".

2. Show the output of the following QuickBASIC program:

```
REM  PROGRAM USING INSTR FUNCTION
LET A$ = "COMPUTER SCIENCE"
LET B$ = "COMPUTE"
PRINT INSTR(1, A$, "C")
PRINT INSTR(1, A$, B$)
PRINT INSTR(1, B$, A$)
PRINT INSTR(1, A$, "E")
LET P = INSTR(1, A$, "E")
REM  TO FIND SECOND E IN A$:
PRINT INSTR(P + 1, A$, "E")
V$ = "THERE WAS NO ROOM IN THE INN."
PRINT INSTR(1, V$, "THE")
PRINT INSTR(1, V$, " THE ")
END
```

3. Show the contents of the array Z$ after the execution of the following QuickBASIC program:

```
DIM Z$(3, 3)
FOR M = 1 TO 3
  FOR J = 1 TO 3
    Z$(M, J) = ""
    FOR K = 1 TO M + J
      Z$(M, J) = Z$(M, J) + "*"
    NEXT K
  NEXT J
NEXT M
END
```

4. Give the exact output provided by the programs below. Indicate any blanks between letters with a lowercase b.

(a)

```
LET A$ = “PEACHES AND HERB”
LET C$ = MID$(A$, 2, 4)
PRINT LEFT$(C$, 4) + “BOWL”
END
```

(b)

```
LET A$ = “”
FOR I = 1 TO 3
   LET A$ = A$ + “ ”
NEXT I
IF A$ = SPACE$(4) PRINT “SAME”
IF A$ <> SPACE$(4) PRINT “DIFFERENT”
END
```

(c)

```
LET A$ = “SPACEY”
FOR I = 1 TO INSTR(1, A$, “A”)
   PRINT MID$(A$, I, 1);
NEXT I
END
```

5. Assume A$ = “UNITED STATES”. Write the output that would result when the following statements are executed. (Consider each statement independently.)

(a) PRINT LEN(A$)

(b) PRINT INSTR(1, A$, “TED”)

(c) PRINT RIGHT$(A$, 9)

(d) PRINT LEFT$(A$, INSTR(1, A$, D))

(e) PRINT MID$(A$, 8, 4) + SPACE$(2) + MID$(A$, 2, 3)

6. Rewrite the lines in the body of the FOR/NEXT loop in Program 32 so that a positive increment is used in the FOR statement to achieve the same results.

7. Modify Program 33 so that INSTR is used to search for MENT rather than MID$ and a FOR/NEXT loop. (*Hint*: Study the two versions of Program 31.)

8. What changes would be necessary in Program 33 so that the output would be words containing the two-letter sequence IS?

E. LAB EXERCISES

1. Suppose your appliance store has a mailing list of customers on file. A record is stored for each individual in a DATA statement that contains a string comprised of the person's name in positions 1–20, the local address in positions 21–40, the city, state, and zip code in positions 41–60, the date of last purchase in 61–68, and the category of the purchase in 69–70. (This category gives information as to what type of appliance was purchased.) For example, you might have customer information stored as follows:

Costello, Annette_ _ _3419 Monroe St_ _ _ _ _ _Bellwood_IL_60104_ _ _10/18/9019

(The underscores are provided here to indicate spaces in the DATA statement.) Reviewing this DATA statement, you see that Annette Costello purchased an item in category 19 on Oct. 18, 1990. As the store manager, you can use the stored information to perform such tasks as

(a) do a general mailing to all customers
(b) use the zip codes to target a geographical region of customers
(c) identify customers who have not shopped in the store for a certain period of time
(d) identify all customers who have purchased a certain type of product

The key to accomplishing any of these tasks is to separate the fields in the record by using string functions. In other words, because the data for Annette Costello is held in a variable, say RECORD$, you will need to extract from RECORD$ various components to perform certain tasks. Write the statement that would select her name and store it in the variable PERSON$.

____

Next, write the statement to select her street address and store it in STREET$.

____

Write the statement to pick out the city, state, and zip code and store it in CITY$.

____

What statement would identify the last date of purchase and store it in LASTP$?

____

Finally, write the statement to store the category number in CATEGORY$.

____

Suppose that you have a reasonably large, but unknown, number of customers. You could follow the list of customers with a trailer of all x's. If this is the approach, what QuickBASIC statements should you use to construct the loop?

____

The condition for loop termination could be

```
PERSON$ < > "xxxxxxxxxxxxxxxxxxxx"
```

Note that the trailer must contain exactly 20 x's.

Now write a short program to take five such records (use the one above and the four listed below), separate the record into its fields, and print out each data item under an appropriate heading. The other four records are

Column 1	21	41	61	69
Adams, Mark	601 Waldron St.	Lafayette, IN 47906	1/7/89	23
Wilson, Deborah	2900 Sienna Ave.	Muncie, IN 47304	7/1/90	1
Fox, Tim	5929 Park St.	Burlington, WI 51624	5/2/90	17
Connors, Mike	1200 Hoyt Ave.	Chicago, IL 60613	11/10/90	35

Write your program below.

2. Modify your program so that instead of printing all of the records, it prints the data for only those customers who have purchased a product in category 19, 23, or 40. Write the modifications in the lines provided.

3. Modify the program you currently have for this lab to print out those customers whose last purchase was made after 12/31/89.

4. Modify the program you currently have for this lab to print out those customers whose zip codes begin with a 4 or a 6.

F. PROGRAMMING PROBLEMS

1. Write a program to count the number of occurrences of the letter *E* in a string A$ of any length.

2. Modify the program you wrote for Problem 1 to count the number of occurrences of the letters *A* or *E* in A$.

3. Write a program that does the following:

   (a) accepts a character string CHAR$ and a word (another character string) WORD$ as input from the user at the terminal,

   (b) determines whether the word WORD$ can be made from the letters supplied in CHAR$. Note, for example, that if WORD$ needs the letter *a* twice and CHAR$ contains only one *a*, then WORD$ *cannot* be formed from CHAR$,

   (c) prints out an appropriate message as to whether or not WORD$ can be formed from CHAR$.

   Your program should allow the user to enter as many pairs of strings (i.e. a CHAR$ and a WORD$) as desired. To test your program, use the following strings as input:

   1. CHAR$ = "abcdef" , WORD$ = "cab"
   2. CHAR$ = "xyz" , WORD$ = "zap"
   3. CHAR$ = "mocpurte" , WORD$ = "compute"
   4. CHAR$ = "abplxe" , WORD$ = "apple"

4. Write a program that accepts two words as input and prints out a listing of those letters common to both words. For example, if CENTER and TELEPHONE are entered, the output should be ENT because these are the letters that appear in both words. The program *should not* print the letter more than once even if it appears more than once in each word (as did the E in the above example). Your program should allow the user to enter as many pairs of words as desired. Test your program with the following pairs of words:

   (a) apple, orange

   (b) strings, harness

   (c) computer, wish

5. Suppose that as part of your business activities, you want to keep a list of all of your current customers. Write a program that searches through an array of names for a name entered at the terminal. To test your program, create an array called LIST$ to hold the following names, which should be read from data statements into your program.

Cathy Cole
Thomas Halvorson
Truly Tye
Robert Higgins
Michael Briddle
Larry Chote
Carol Wiggins
Michelle Scribner

After accepting a name and performing the search, your program should either print a message stating that the name is in your list of customers or a message that the name needs to be added to the list. (This type of application can also be handled with files, and will be revisited in Chapter Seven, Program 40.)

6. Write a program to read lines of text and then count the number of words, number of characters, and the number of occurrences of the single-character word *a*. Use the six-line paragraph that describes Step 1 for Program 31 as the data for this problem. (It begins "Just for the fun of it...".) Some guidelines are:

   (a) Use a six-cell character string array called LINE$ to hold the six lines of text.

   (b) Use a repetition structure to read each line, a character at a time, and count the number of words, characters, and occurrences of the word *a*. Even though a blank is a real ASCII character, do not include blanks in your count of characters. (We're taking what might be thought of as a layman's view of a character as only that which can be seen on the printed page.)

   (c) You'll need to search for a character string more than one character in length to find the occurrences of the word *a*. You'll also have to modify your search technique to consider the cases where *a* is the first or last character of a line.

7. As you may have noticed, acronyms are very common in computer science and in everyday life. Some examples are:

   Horizontal Software Marketing: HSM
   A Programming Language: APL
   Cabbies for the Advancement of Dental Surgery: CADS
   Beginners All-Purpose Symbolic Instruction Code: BASIC
   Internal Revenue Service: IRS

   For this project, you are to use QuickBASIC string manipulation functions to write a program that creates acronyms. Here are some specifics about how the program should be written:

   (a) The input should be a name or phrase that is a string of words separated by one or more blanks. The words may begin with uppercase or lowercase letters.

   (b) If the first letter of a word is uppercase, it should be included in the acronym.

   (c) The method of looking for letters to be included in the acronym should go something like this:

1. Look for occurrences of blanks in the string and use the next character in the string as a potential letter in the acronym.
2. A letter may be included in the acronym if and only if it is an uppercase letter and not a blank.
3. Once all blanks have been found, the program is finished.

(d) To help make the above method work, a blank character should be inserted at the beginning of the input string so that the first uppercase letter will be found.

(e) Hint: use the INSTR function to look for the occurrences of blanks in the input string.

Here are examples of what a run would look like:

Enter a name or phrase? National Association for the Advancement of Colored People
Acronym = NAACP

Enter a name or phrase? Association for Computing Machinery
Acronym = ACM

8. A group of CS majors got together the other day and typed in a Christmas song. They weren't very original. Also, it seems that they have a problem with a few little things (such as capitalization). So, they are requesting your help. Here is the song they typed:

"Jingle bells. jingle bells. jingle all the way."
"oh what fun it is to ride in a one horse"
"open sleigh. hey. jingle bells. jingle bells."

Notice that they forgot the capitalization at the beginning of almost all of the sentences. Your task is to write a program that reads in the song (the song should be in three DATA statements). Then find all of the periods in each line. Two blank spaces always follow the periods (the CS majors do follow this convention). In other words, three characters after the period is a letter that should be capitalized. Here is a formula that you can put on the right side of a user-defined function that changes a lowercase letter into an uppercase letter:

CHR$(ASC(X$)-32)

where X$ is a variable that holds a single character.

And so you need to substitute the lowercase letter with an uppercase letter and still preserve the rest of the line.

Hints:

(a) INSTR can be used to find the periods. Be sure to check the value of the starting position.

1. String constant form:

   PRINT USING "format", expression list

The statement tells the computer to use the particular format specified to print the expression(s) listed.

2. String expression form:

   LET N$ = "format"
   PRINT USING N$, expression list

This option is useful if N$ is a complicated format used in many PRINT USING statements in a given program. It is much simpler to type "N$" than the entire format over and over. (Of course N$ could be replaced by any other character string variable here.)

The format that is used in both of the above forms contains special control characters which result in specific output images. The format control characters are listed in Table 6.1.

Format Control Character	Use	Examples
#	Used with numeric data, one symbol for each digit to be printed. If a decimal point is included, pads with zeros to the right of the decimal point.	####
**	Leading asterisks; i.e., fills a field to the first digit with asterisks. Useful in check protection applications.	**##.##
$	Fixed dollar sign. Causes a dollar sign to be printed exactly as specified.	$###.##
$$	Floating dollar sign. Causes a dollar sign to be printed just to the left of the first digit.	$$##.##
,	Comma insertion. Places a comma after every three digits starting at decimal point and proceeding to the left.	##,###.##
-	Trailing negative sign. Negative numbers will have a minus sign appearing to the right of the number.	###.## -
\\(*n*-2 spaces)\\	Specifies an *n*-character-wide field for alphanumeric data, pads on right with blanks.	_ _ _\\

Table 6.1 Format Control Characters

Examples using these control characters follow. For simplicity, the output that would result from executing the statement(s) in each example is given immediately following the line(s) of code. Blanks in a field are indicated again by underscores.

<u>Examples</u>

1. PRINT USING "########"; 382

_____382

This example uses the string constant form. The number appears right justified in a field eight characters in length.

2. LET N$ = "########"
   PRINT USING N$; 382

_____382

The string expression form is used here. The output is exactly the same as in example 1.

3. LET N$ = "#####"
   PRINT USING N$; 382, 4675

__382_4675

In this example, the numbers appear right justified in consecutive five-character fields on the same print line. Note that the comma is simply used to separate the items in the expression list.

4. PRINT USING "###"; 8
   PRINT USING "###"; 96
   PRINT USING "###"; 378

__8
_96
378

The output is right justified in a field three characters long.

5. PRINT USING "###"; 86.37
PRINT USING "###"; 95
PRINT USING "###"; 4146

```
 _ 86
 _ 95
 %4146
```

This format specifies a field of length 3, with no digits to the right of the decimal point. Therefore, when printing 86.37, no decimal digits are allowed and the output is 86. The number 4146 is too large for the field specified, and so an overflow symbol, the percent sign, appears along with the entire number as shown.

6. A$ = "###.##"
PRINT USING A$; 319.6
PRINT USING A$; -27.94
PRINT USING A$; 85.236
PRINT USING A$; -325

```
319.60
-27.94
_85.24
%-325.00
```

Several interesting results appear here. Note that when two decimal places are specified in the format, two digits always appear to the right of the decimal point in the output (unless overflow occurs). Thus in the first case a zero is provided to fill the field and print 319.60. The second number shows that a negative sign takes one space in the field, which is also the reason the attempt to print -325 results in overflow. The format given by A$ allows only two digits to the right of the decimal point. When more occur, as in 85.236, rounding takes place and you see the output as 85.24. Finally, note the alignment of decimal points for numbers that do not result in overflow.

7. PRINT USING "**###.##"; 36
PRINT USING "**###.##"; 136.4
PRINT USING "**###.##"; 1136.45
PRINT USING "**###.##"; 21136.45

```
***36.00
**136.40
*1136.45
21136.45
```

The format here specifies that the field should fill with asterisks, allow two digits to the right of the decimal point, and allow a maximum value of 99999.99 to be printed. Note again the zero fill and the alignment of decimal points.

8. LET A$ = "$####.##"
   PRINT USING A$; 36
   PRINT USING A$; 136.4
   PRINT USING A$; 1136.45
   PRINT USING A$; 21136.45

```
$ _ _ 3 6 . 0 0
$ _ 1 3 6 . 4 0
$ 1 1 3 6 . 4 5
$ % 2 1 1 3 6 . 4 5
```

This example shows the use of the fixed dollar sign, which results in dollar signs aligned vertically. Note that when the dollar amount 136.4 is printed, it appears in the preferred form 136.40. A dollar sign must appear in the output for each number.

9. A$ = "$$###.##"
   PRINT USING A$; 36
   PRINT USING A$; 136.4
   PRINT USING A$; 1136.45
   PRINT USING A$; 21136.45

```
_ _ $ 3 6 . 0 0
_ $ 1 3 6 . 4 0
$ 1 1 3 6 . 4 5
% $ 2 1 1 3 6 . 4 5
```

Using two dollar signs in the format results in the floating dollar sign. Again, one dollar sign must appear with each number.

10. A$ = "##,###.##"
    PRINT USING A$; 326.94
    PRINT USING A$; 1753.623
    PRINT USING A$; 29.37

```
_ _ _ 3 2 6 . 9 4
_ 1 , 7 5 3 . 6 2
_ _ _ _ 2 9 . 3 7
```

This format calls for a comma to be inserted between the third and fourth digits from and to the left of the decimal point. If the number has three or fewer digits to the left of the decimal point, then no comma will be printed.

11. A$ = "###.## -"
    PRINT USING A$; 31.92
    PRINT USING A$; -45.68
    PRINT USING A$; -426.935

```
_ 3 1 . 9 2
_ 4 5 . 6 8  -
4 2 6 . 9 3  -
```

Here a trailing negative sign is used to highlight in the rightmost column of the field the numbers that are negative.

12. A$ = "$**##.##"
    PRINT USING A$; 23.85
    PRINT USING A$; 36
    PRINT USING A$; 216.46
    PRINT USING A$; 4196.23

```
$ * * 2 3 . 8 5
$ * * 3 6 . 0 0
$ * 2 1 6 . 4 6
$ 4 1 9 6 . 2 3
```

The fixed dollar sign and the fill with asterisks are used here to display currency amounts.

13. A$ = "$$#,###.##-"
    PRINT USING A$; 239.65
    PRINT USING A$, 4192.78
    PRINT USING A$; 98714.36
    PRINT USING A$; -1.23
    PRINT USING A$; .46

```
_ _ _ $ 2 3 9 . 6 5
_ $ 4 , 1 9 2 . 7 8
$ 9 8 , 7 1 4 . 3 6
_ _ _ _ _ $ 1 . 2 3  -
_ _ _ _ _ $ 0 . 4 6
```

In this example, A$ provides a floating dollar sign, comma insertion, and a trailing negative sign, with a maximum value of $99,999.99. If the format expression were A$ = "$$#,###.##", then the number -1.23 would be printed as

```
_ _ _ _ - $ 1 . 2 3
```

14. A$ = "_ _ _\"
    PRINT USING A$; "JANE"
    PRINT USING A$; "ROBINSON"

J A N E _ _
R O B I N S

This format is used to specify a field length for alphanumeric data. Note that truncation occurs when the string is longer than the formatted field.

15. A$ = "JANE"
    B$ = "_ _ _ _ _ _\"
    PRINT USING B$; SPACE$(LEN(B$)/2 - INT(LEN(A$)/2)) + A$

_ _ J A N E _ _

The print statement displays JANE centered in a field of length 8. Note that the argument of SPACE$ evaluates to the value 2 in this example. (A negative argument for SPACE$, which would happen in the PRINT statement if the length of A$ is greater than 8, results in the display of an error message.)

16. A$ = "_ _ _ _ _ _\ $$###.##"
    PRINT USING A$; "JANE", 27.43

JANE _ _ _ _ _ _ $27.43

"JANE" appears left justified in a field of length 8. Two of the six spaces before the dollar sign are a result of positions not used in displaying the dollar amount.

17. N = 319.27
    A$ = "_ _ _ _ _ _\" + SPACE$(5) + "$$###.##"
    PRINT USING A$; "SUM IS", N

SUM _ IS _ _ _ _ _ _ _ _ $319.27

Note that concatenation is used here to construct the format A$.

D. USING TAB AND PRINT USING IN PROGRAMS

To see how the TAB function and the PRINT USING statement can be effective in programs, let us begin by enhancing the output of Program 21 from Chapter Three. This program, the car rental problem, resulted in the output of three columns of data, with headings, using the standard print zones. Note that the headings were not equally spaced, the numbers were not centered under the headings, the decimal points were not aligned, zero fill was not used in the dollar amounts, and the dollar signs for the cost data were omitted. All of these deficiencies can be remedied by using the TAB function and the PRINT USING statement as shown below.

Program 35.

```
'PROGRAM TO DETERMINE CAR RENTAL COSTS WHICH ARE BASED ON
'THE NUMBER OF MILES DRIVEN.  A FUNCTION CALLED CHARGE IS USED
'TO CALCULATE THE COST FOR EACH OF TEN RENTALS.  A PRINT USING
'STATEMENT FORMATS THE OUTPUT.

'************* PRINT HEADING ************************
PRINT "RENTAL #"; TAB(14); "MILES"; TAB(25); "COST"

'********** PROCESS THE CAR RENTALS ***************
A$ = "####" + SPACE$(8) + "####.#" + SPACE$(5) + "$###.##"
FOR RENTAL = 1 TO 10
  READ MILES
  PRINT USING A$; RENTAL, MILES, CHARGE(MILES)
NEXT RENTAL
DATA 320, 605, 407.6, 394.2, 501
DATA 560.4, 480, 540, 402.7, 420
END

FUNCTION CHARGE(MILES)
IF MILES <= 400 THEN
  CHARGE = 75
ELSEIF MILES=INT(MILES) THEN
  CHARGE = 75 + .2 * (MILES-400)
ELSE
  CHARGE = 75 + .2 * (INT(MILES - 400) + 1)
END IF
END FUNCTION
```

Output:

```
RENTAL #        MILES       COST
    1           320.0     $ 75.00
    2           605.0     $116.00
    3           407.6     $ 76.60
    4           394.2     $ 75.00
    5           501.0     $ 95.20
    6           560.4     $107.20
    7           480.0     $ 91.00
    8           540.0     $103.00
    9           402.7     $ 75.60
   10           420.0     $ 79.00
```

Compare the output of Program 35 to that of Program 21.

Program 36.

Step 1. Describe the problem.

A common business application where you can use the TAB function and the PRINT USING statement is for printing out a formatted monthly checking account summary. The beginning balance, each debit and credit, and an ending balance should be displayed.

Step 2. Design the logic of the solution.

You'll want to show check amounts as a debit by using a trailing negative sign and deposits as a credit (with no sign). Because you do not know the number of transactions that will take place, use a WHILE/WEND loop and a trailer of 0 for the value of the variable AMOUNT to signal the end of the transactions.

Step 3. Code the program.

```
REM MONTHLY CHECKING ACCOUNT TRANSACTIONS
CLS
REM ******** READ AND PRINT BEGINNING BALANCE *********************
READ BALANCE
A$ = "\___________________\"+SPACE$(13)+"$$####.##"
B$ = "\______\"+SPACE$(6)+'$$####.##-"+SPACE$(7)+"$$####.##-"
PRINT USING A$; "BEGINNING BALANCE",BALANCE
PRINT
PRINT "DATE";TAB(15);"TRANSACTION";TAB(34);"BALANCE"

REM *********** PROCESS TRANSACTIONS **********************************
READ DAY$, AMOUNT
WHILE AMOUNT<>0
  BALANCE = BALANCE + AMOUNT
  PRINT USING B$;DAY$,AMOUNT,BALANCE
  READ DAY$, AMOUNT
WEND

REM ****** PRINT ENDING BALANCE **************************************
PRINT
PRINT USING A$; "ENDING BALANCE",BALANCE
DATA 464.30
DATA 08/08/90,-135,08/04/90,300,07/30/90,-25.60,07/27/90,-12.99
DATA 09/12/90,-16.33,09/09/90,-56.25,08/17/90,-90.66
DATA 09/01/90,150,09/14/90,-275,10/03/90,-90.5
DATA "1/1/91", 0
END
```

Output:

```
BEGINNING BALANCE              $464.30

 DATE      TRANSACTION       BALANCE
08/08/90     $135.00-        $329.30
08/04/90     $300.00         $629.30
07/30/90      $25.60-        $603.70
07/27/90      $12.99-        $590.71
09/12/90      $16.33-        $574.38
09/09/90      $56.25-        $518.13
08/17/90      $90.66-        $427.47
09/01/90     $150.00         $577.47
09/14/90     $275.00-        $302.47
10/03/90      $90.50-        $211.97

ENDING BALANCE                 $211.97
```

Further Notes on Program 36:

1. The values of the TAB function in the PRINT statement are found by experimentation. After several tries, it was determined that 15 and 39 give the desired output.

2. Note that when 0 is to be read in for AMOUNT, a date must also be read. The date 1/1/91 was chosen arbitrarily. The variable DAY$ is used because the more obvious choice DATE$ is a reserved word in QuickBASIC.

E. REVIEW EXERCISES

1. Run example 15 on your computer with B$ nine characters instead of eight characters long. Is the extra space printed before or after JANE?

2. Referring again to example 15, what would be the result if the concatenation operator (+) was replaced with a semicolon?

3. Determine the columns in which the output from lines 30 and 40 would begin and end.

```
LET T$ = "COMPUTING IS EASY"
LET R$ = "FOR ME"
PRINT TAB(15); T$
PRINT TAB(10); T$; TAB(30); R$
END
```

4. Show the output of the following programs. Be sure to indicate blanks!

(a)
```
LET A = 123.4567
LET B = -31.76
LET H$ = "###.##"
PRINT USING H$; A
PRINT USING H$; B
END
```

(b)
```
PRINT USING "###.###"; 1234.5678, -4.5678
END
```

(c)
```
LET H$ = "$###.##" + SPACE$(5) + "\_ _ _ _ _ _\"
PRINT USING H$; 402.2, "ADAMS"
PRINT USING H$; 658, "WILSON"
END
```

(d)
```
LET A = -12.34
LET B = 12.123
LET H$ = "$**#.##-"
PRINT USING H$; A
PRINT USING H$; B
END
```

(e)
```
PRINT USING "$$###.##"; 400
PRINT USING "$$###.##"; 796.7
PRINT USING "$$###.##"; 12403.41
END
```

F. LAB EXERCISE

In this lab, you will create a salespersons' salary and company sales report. You will design the program and develop the formatting specifications step by step. Assume that there are eight salespersons, each making a monthly base salary plus a percentage of their total sales for that month. The following data statements give each individual's name, monthly base pay, commission percentage, and sales for the month.

```
DATA Tom Jones, 2000, 7, 3175.80
DATA Alice Wilson, 2400, 15, 4120
DATA Elizabeth Ann Alexander, 1800, 6, 2565.93
DATA Brad Livingston, 2150, 8, 1267.90
DATA John Frankton, 2600, 10, 3112
DATA Michael Thomas, 1800, 7, 0
```

DATA Mary Alice Wilson, 2500, 11, 3708.60
DATA Deborah Wage, 2200, 7.5, 2765.71

You will read these data into the variables SALESPERSON, BASE, COMM, and SALES, respectively. Of course, you'll need to establish a reasonable format to display each of these, using a single formatting string A$. Suppose the name of a salesperson is no more than 20 characters long. Write the first part of A$, which will hold a salesperson's name.

(a) ____

Next assume that the monthly base pay is no more than $9999 and is a whole dollar amount. Write the appropriate format to display these values, using a floating dollar sign.

(b) ____

The commission percentage is read as an integer instead of as a decimal value (e.g., 7% commission is given by the value 7, not .07). Write the format to hold commission values as high as 15%.

(c) ____

Monthly sales will also be displayed. Write the format so that these values can be as large as $99,999.99. Use a floating dollar sign, two decimal places, and zero fill.

(d) ____

To display the total monthly salary, you'll want a format to handle up to five digits to the left of the decimal point, a fixed dollar sign, zero fill, two digits to the right of the decimal point, and asterisks filling blank spaces. Write the appropriate formatting description.

(e) ____

Now combine formats (a), (b), (c), (d) and (e) into A$, putting five spaces between entries. Write the string expression below.

____

Each person's total salary must be calculated and stored in a variable, say TOTAL. Write the expression to perform this calculation using the variables TOTAL, BASE, COMM, and SALES. Be sure to modify the commission percentage (i.e., 7% must be entered as .07).

____

You'll use a FOR/NEXT loop to process the eight salespersons' data. You'll also want to calculate the total company sales for the month and the average base pay for the eight salespersons. Thus you'll need two more statements within your loop, one to accumulate total base pay and another to sum the total company sales. Use TOTALBASE and COMPSALES for these tasks.

The inside of the loop now consists of a READ statement, a calculation of each person's TOTAL pay, a PRINT USING statement, and the calculations of TOTALBASE and COMPSALES. Write A$ and the loop below.

After the loop, you'll need to calculate the average base pay for the salespersons. Write the statement that calculates AVGBASE.

Finally, you'll print out the average base salary and the total company sales, employing a PRINT USING statement. Create a string expression B$ to "hold" the messages "AVERAGE BASE SALARY" and "TOTAL COMPANY SALES", skip 15 spaces, and then print out the corresponding values. Assume that these values may have as many as six digits to the left of the decimal point and allow for a floating dollar sign and zero fill. Write B$ below.

Enter into your computer your entire program, paying careful attention to the syntax of your formatting strings, A$ and B$, and to your PRINT USING statements. Run your program and modify it if necessary.

As you examine your output, notice what happened to Elizabeth Ann's name. How can this problem be remedied? Write the necessary change below.

G. PROGRAMMING PROBLEMS

1. In Programming Problem 1 of Chapter Two, the output was a 30-day pay schedule. Using the TAB function and the PRINT USING statement, modify this program so that the output has the following characteristics:

   (a) column headings are equally spaced (10 spaces),

   (b) numbers are centered in each column,

   (c) decimal positions are aligned,

   (d) dollar signs are used when appropriate,

   (e) the total pay for the month is aligned with the dollar amounts shown in the third column.

2. Modify Programming Problem 4 of Chapter Two, where a four-column display showing office purchases and prices was the output, so that it too has characteristics (a) through (e) listed in Programming Problem 1 and also

(f) zero fill is used with dollar amounts.

3. In Review Exercise 9 of Chapter Two, a program was given to print out selections and prices of items chosen at the Dumpy Burger Restaurant. Modify this program so that the output simulates a cash register receipt having characteristics (c), (d), and (f) listed above. Be sure the total cost of the order is aligned properly.

4. Modify Program 9 of this text, where various monthly car payments were displayed, so that the output has characteristics (a), (c), and (d) listed above.

5. Write a program to print the numbers 1.1, 10.01, 100.001, and 1000.0001 so that the decimal points are aligned and occur in column 25 on the page.

6. Modify Program 36 to incorporate the following characteristics. In your program, use the information that on January 1 the account balance was $1000 and during the month of January the following transactions took place:

January 3	withdrawal	$325.20
January 5	withdrawal	18.00
January 8	deposit	400.00
January 12	withdrawal	88.60
January 18	withdrawal	225.00
January 23	withdrawal	47.83
January 26	deposit	150.00
January 30	withdrawal	22.00

Your program should

(a) Enter the value 1000 into the program using an assignment statement.

(b) Use a code of 1 to indicate a deposit, 2 to indicate a withdrawal, and 3 to stop the program.

(c) Based on the code, branch to an appropriate set of statements using a SELECT CASE statement.

(d) Use READ/DATA statements to enter the code and the dollar amounts.

(e) Use the TAB function and PRINT USING statement to output a table with headings showing the date, the deposit or withdrawal, and the current balance. Be sure to align decimal points, print dollar signs, use comma insertion, and fill with zeros when appropriate. Also, the numbers should be centered under each heading.

(f) Print a message if the balance is less than 0.

7. A cruise line service estimates that its revenue for a given cruise must be $10,000 to break even. Its standard travel package to groups of vacationers is as follows. A minimum of 20 people must go on the cruise at a cost of $500 per person. For every additional person who signs up, the cost per person is reduced by $10. Write a program to display a table that shows the cost per customer and the profit for the cruise line when the number of customers varies from 20 to 40. Also print a message indicating the number of customers that will maximize the company's profit. Use column headings and format the values appropriately in the center of each column.

8. In Chapter Four, Programming Problem 7, you were asked to write a program to aid in controlling inventory related to the production of Whirly Disks. For this problem, enhance that program so that

   (a) inventory numbers at each warehouse are right justified in each column.

   (b) dollar signs and zero fill are used with monetary amounts.

   (c) decimal positions are aligned.

   (d) column headings are equally spaced (five spaces).

CHAPTER SEVEN

DATA FILES

"*All which thy child's mistake fancies as lost, I have stored for thee at home.*" (Francis Thompson, 1859–1907, *The Hound of Heaven*, Stanza 5.)

A. INTRODUCTION

Up to now, you have used three different methods of entering data into a program. These are the LET statement, the INPUT statement, and the READ/DATA combination of statements. When a considerable amount of data needs to be processed, the preferred choice is the READ/DATA combination. However, there are situations involving large amounts of data for which these statements are inadequate. For example, if the same data needs to be accessed by several programs, it would be very inefficient to type the same DATA statements into each program. For this reason, QuickBASIC has a fourth method for entering data into a program, namely through the use of data files. A data file can be created through a QuickBASIC program and stored on a peripheral device (secondary storage) for later use. Because the data file resides external to any QuickBASIC program, it can be made available to more than one applications program.

The QuickBASIC statements that are used in file processing include OPEN, PRINT #, CLOSE, and INPUT #. To write data to a file and later access the data for use in a program, you proceed as follows:

OPEN	establishes a communication link between a program and a data file either to create a file to accept output from a program or to read data from a file into a program.
PRINT #	writes data to a file that has been opened for output.
CLOSE	closes the communication link between a program and a file. If a file is open for output, a CLOSE must be issued before the file can be reOPENed for input.
INPUT #	reads information from a file into a program.

Figure 7.1 depicts the relationship between a program in main memory and a data file in secondary storage. When a data file is created through a QuickBASIC program, we can say that data is written to the file (as opposed to being printed on paper or on a terminal screen.) When data from a file is used in a program, the data is read from the file.

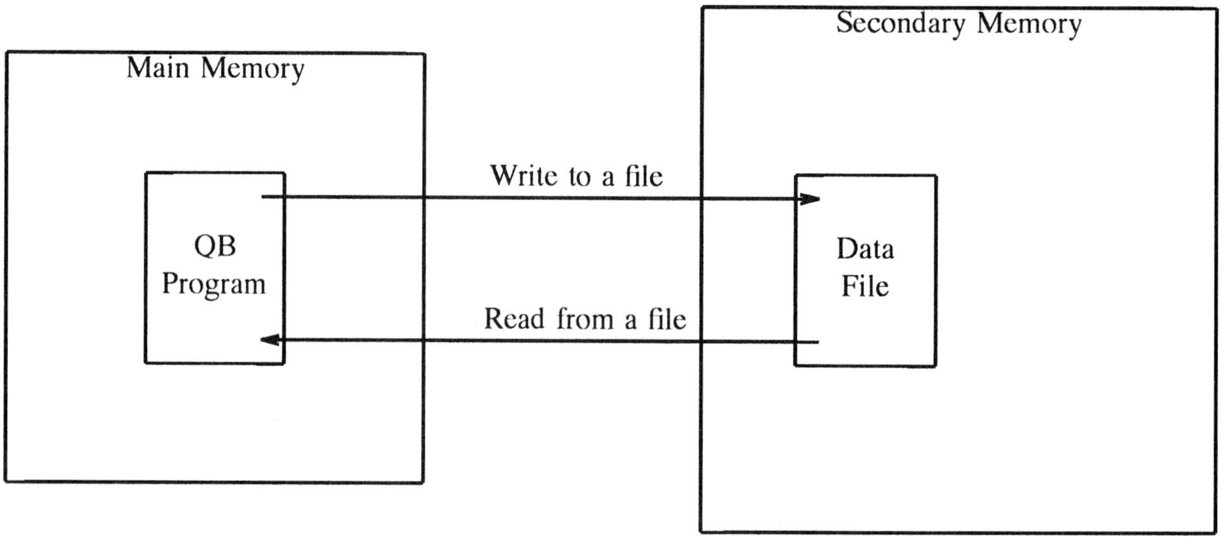

Figure 7.1. Writing to and Reading from a Data File

What Is a File?

A *data file* is a named collection of related data residing in secondary storage. For example, a computer science teacher may have a file called CS110 for his introductory computer science class. This file would contain a record for each student, and in turn, each record would contain several fields holding data about that student. Thus, the file CS110 might have a record for Janet Allison in which there are fields for Janet's name, identification number, score on test 1, score on quiz 1, 2, and 3, and so on. This data hierarchy is displayed in Figure 7.2.

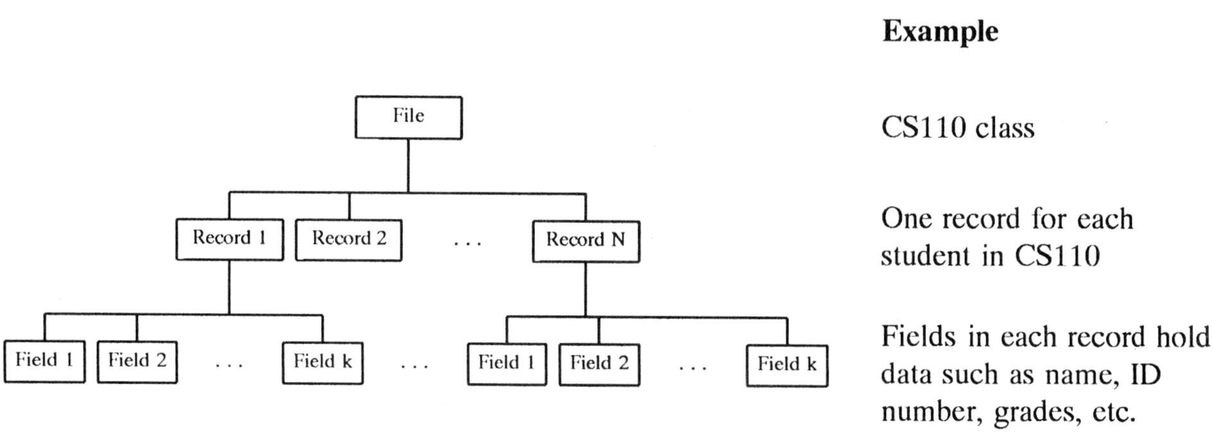

Figure 7.2 The Data Hierarchy

A computer can access a file in a sequential manner or in a random (non-sequential) manner. In this text, only sequential files are considered. In such files, the records are in sequence and have to be accessed in order, one after another. Thus to access one particular record in the middle of a file, the computer must read through all of the previous records to arrive at the desired record.

In this chapter, methods for creating, using, and updating sequential data files are discussed.

B. WRITING TO AND READING FROM FILES

To open a communication link between a QuickBASIC program and a data file to be used for input or output, the OPEN statement is used. Its general form is

```
OPEN "filename" FOR OUTPUT AS # file designator
OPEN "filename" FOR INPUT AS # file designator
```

When a file is opened for OUTPUT, data can be written to the specified file in secondary storage. OPENing a file that already exists for OUTPUT will cause that file to be replaced by whatever is written to it from a program. When a file is opened for INPUT, data can be read from the file into a program. The *file designator* at the end of each of the above statements is a number used in the QuickBASIC program to refer to that particular file. Consider the following examples. The OPEN statement below establishes a data file to accept bowlers' names and league averages.

```
OPEN "BOWL" FOR OUTPUT AS #1
```

To use the data file BOWL to read data into a program, you could write

```
OPEN "BOWL" FOR INPUT AS #3
```

(The file number can range from 1 to 255 in QuickBASIC. The choices of 1 and 3 here have no special significance.)

The next program creates the file BOWL. The names and averages of three bowlers are entered from the terminal.

Program 37.

```
OPEN "BOWL" FOR OUTPUT AS #1
PRINT "ENTER NAME AND AVERAGE"
INPUT BOWLER$, AVE
WHILE BOWLER$ < > "END"
 PRINT #1, BOWLER$
 PRINT #1, AVE
 INPUT BOWLER$, AVE
WEND
CLOSE 1
END
```

Sample Output:

ENTER NAME AND AVERAGE
? WILSON, 181
? MYERS, 193
? ROTH, 201
? END, 0

Further Notes on Program 37:

1. The OPEN statement names the file BOWL and gives it the number 1 as the file designator.
2. In response to the INPUT statement, the user types in a name and number, separated by a comma.
3. The trailer used here is "END". In the output listed above, the number 0 also was entered to satisfy the input requirements of the INPUT statement. Of course, any number other than 0 would also suffice.
4. The PRINT statement causes the output to be written to file #1, (i.e., to the file BOWL, rather than on the terminal or on a printer). Note that the name of the file, BOWL, appears only once in the program.
5. The CLOSE statement terminates the communication link between the QuickBASIC program and the data file BOWL. The file is also saved for future use.
6. To see the file BOWL, you can pull down the File menu, select the Open Program option and then type in your selection, namely "BOWL." (type the period, too). The file will look like the following:

   WILSON
   181
   MYERS
   193
   ROTH
   201

   The next program uses the file BOWL that was just created.

Program 38.

This program simply prints out the three names and corresponding averages from the file BOWL.

```
OPEN "BOWL" FOR INPUT AS #3
FOR I = 1 TO 3
  INPUT #3, BOWLER$
  INPUT #3, AVE
  PRINT BOWLER$, AVE
NEXT I
CLOSE 3
END
```

Output:

WILSON	181
MYERS	193
ROTH	201

Notes on Program 38:

1. Each time the INPUT statements are encountered, a value is read from the file BOWL. Note that each INPUT statement uses the same file designator (3) as was established in the OPEN statement. These two statements can be replaced by the single INPUT statement

   INPUT #3, BOWLER$, AVE

2. Once values are read from the file into BOWLER$ and AVE, they can be printed out using any of the formatting techniques that you have seen. Here, commas are used in the PRINT statement to dislay the data in the first and second print zones.
3. Files used for INPUT must also be closed.

Of course the writing to a file and the reading from a file can be accomplished in the same program. Consider the next example, paying special attention to how the data is written to the file and read back into the program.

Program 39.

Step 1. Describe the problem.

You want to create a data file which is to contain the name, age, and rank in the corporation (given by a number in the range 1 to 10, with 1 representing the highest level in the corporation) of the employee. For our purposes here, you will use data for five individuals. After creating the file, you want to print out the file to be sure that there are no errors in the data.

Step 2. Design the logic of the solution.

Start by opening a file called EMPLOYEE for output. After all of the data is entered from the terminal, close this output file and then use a second OPEN statement in which you establish this same file as the input file. After data is read into the program and printed out, close the file a second time.

Step 3. Code the program.

```
REM  PROGRAM TO CREATE THE FILE
REM  EMPLOYEE AND PRINT OUT ITS CONTENTS

REM *******CREATE FILE WITH 5 EMPLOYEES ********
OPEN "EMPLOYEE" FOR OUTPUT AS #1
PRINT "ENTER NAME, AGE, AND RANK"
FOR I = 1 TO 5
  INPUT PERSON$, AGE, RANK
  PRINT #1, PERSON$; ","; AGE; ","; RANK
NEXT I
CLOSE 1

REM ***** PRINT THE CONTENTS OF THE FILE ********
OPEN "EMPLOYEE" FOR INPUT AS #2
PRINT "NAME", "AGE", "RANK"
PRINT
FOR I = 1 TO 5
  INPUT #2, PERSON$, A, R
  PRINT PERSON$, A, R
NEXT I
CLOSE 2
END
```

Sample Output:

```
ENTER NAME, AGE, AND RANK
? THOMAS, 48, 3
? ALLISON, 60, 2
? ANDREWS, 37, 5
? MATHEWS, 29, 7
? ROBERTS, 56, 2

NAME                 AGE              RANK

THOMAS               48               3
ALLISON              60               2
ANDREWS              37               5
MATHEWS              29               7
ROBERTS              56               2
```

Further Notes on Program 39:

1. Note that the PRINT # statement prints commas in the data file. Commas need to be inserted into the data file to separate string data items and combinations of string and numeric data items that are written to the file on the same line (much like commas

separating data in a DATA statement). More generally, commas and an end of a line delimit string data, whereas commas, spaces and an end of a line delimit numeric data.

2. Because three data items are written to the file through one execution of the PRINT # statement, they must be entered back into the program with one execution of an INPUT # statement. You can visualize this file as having three data items per line.
3. The first INPUT statement, where the user enters data from a terminal, has no effect on how the data is written to the file or read from the file. In fact, if this statement were replaced with the following statements, the results of the program would be the same.

```
INPUT PERSON$
INPUT AGE
INPUT RANK
```

4. The file designator number changed from 1 to 2 as the file EMPLOYEE changed from an output to an input file. The input file number could have just as easily remained a 1. Note that the CLOSE statements each refer to the appropriate file designator.
5. PERSON$, A and R are the variable names used in the second part of the program. Of course, when the data is read from the file into the program, it can be put into any legal variable that you choose.

QuickBASIC allows you to reset the pointer back to the beginning of a sequential input data file using the RESET statement. Although this option is available in QuickBASIC, you can still reset the pointer by closing and reopening the input file.

Searching For a Name in a Data File

Consider the following program:

```
OPEN “NAMES” FOR OUTPUT AS #1
LET FULLNAME$ – “DAVIS, TOM”
PRINT #1, FULLNAME$
CLOSE 1
OPEN “NAMES” FOR INPUT AS #1
INPUT #1, FULLNAME$
PRINT FULLNAME$
CLOSE 1
END
```

You might expect the output from the PRINT statement in this program to be

DAVIS, TOM

However, this is not the case. Quotation marks are not printed on files. Therefore, although DAVIS, TOM is in the file, this entry is understood by the computer to be two data items separated by a comma. Thus when data from the file is read into the program, FULLNAME$ is assigned the value DAVIS and this is all that is printed when this program is executed.

One way to output DAVIS, TOM is to modify the above program using two variables in the following way:

```
INPUT #1, LAST$, FIRST$
PRINT LAST$; ","; FIRST$
```

These INPUT statements assign DAVIS to LAST$ and TOM to FIRST$, which results in the PRINT statement displaying the last name, a comma, and the first name.

Having made these preliminary remarks, let us now search for a name in a data file.

Program 40.

Step 1. Describe the problem.

A data file called NAMES is to be searched for a particular name that will be entered at the terminal. The output is to be a message as to whether or not the name is in the data file.

Step 2. Design the logic of the solution.

The assumption here is that the file NAMES already exists with the names entered last name first, with at least one entry in the file. There seems to be a problem because the number of names in the file is not known. However, QuickBASIC supplies an end-of-file indicator (EOF) that you can use to determine if the end of a sequential file has been reached. You will check if the last name and first name entered are equal to the last and first names in any record in the file.

Step 3. Code the program.

```
REM  PROGRAM TO SEARCH FOR A NAME IN
REM  A DATA FILE CALLED NAMES
OPEN "NAMES" FOR INPUT AS #1
PRINT "WHAT NAME ARE YOU SEARCHING FOR?"
PRINT "ENTER LAST NAME, A COMMA, THEN FIRST NAME."
INPUT LAST$, FIRST$
INPUT #1, X$, Y$
WHILE NOT EOF(1) AND NOT(X$ = LAST$ AND Y$ = FIRST$)
  INPUT #1, X$, Y$
WEND
IF X$ = LAST$ AND Y$ = FIRST$ THEN
   PRINT LAST$;","; FIRST$; "IS IN THE FILE"
ELSE
   PRINT LAST$;",";FIRST$;"IS NOT IN THE FILE"
END IF
CLOSE
END
```

Further Notes on Program 40:

1. EOF(1) informs the program when the end of file 1 has been reached. It allows you to not have to worry about how many data entries are in the file.
2. Of course, for this program to work correctly, the full name must be entered exactly as indicated.
3. The logical expression in the WHILE statement tells the program to keep searching for a name while there are still entries to check and while LAST$ *and* FIRST$ have not been found.
4. It was already mentioned that the program assumes that at least one entry is in the file. How is this assumption used in the program? What would happen if the file was empty?
5. There is an alternative to entering the last name into X$ and the first name into Y$ as done above. If the name is originally written to the file without a comma, say DAVIS TOM, then it can be read into the program into just one string variable X$. If this were the case, then Program 40 would need the following modifications:

```
PRINT "ENTER LAST NAME, A SPACE, THEN FIRST NAME."
INPUT PERSON$
INPUT #1, X$
WHILE NOT EOF(1) AND NOT(X$ = PERSON$)
  INPUT #1, X$
WEND
IF X$=PERSON$ THEN
   PRINT PERSON$; "IS IN THE FILE"
ELSE
   PRINT PERSON$;"IS NOT IN THE FILE"
END IF
```

6. The CLOSE statement used without an argument will close all data files opened in a program.

C. FILE MAINTENANCE

A common application of data files is updating existing files. Names need to be added or deleted from customer lists, quantities of specific inventory items change every day, expenditure totals must be updated periodically, and student test results are inserted into existing grade files. In this section, it is shown that file maintenance is possible with sequential files.

Program 41.

Step 1. Describe the problem.

Suppose the company Computers International (CI) retains a list of its customers in a data file called CLIENTS. Each record in the file contains the customer's name and the number of purchases made from CI. (To simplify matters, you will use only last names for customers and assume that there are no more than 100 customers at the present time.) This week the company finds that not only have some of its previous customers purchased new computers, but also that it has acquired several new customers. You want to write a program that will update the existing file CLIENTS.

Step 2. Design the logic of the solution.

Each customer is associated with a number of purchases made. The easiest way to update the records is to read them from the file CLIENTS into arrays. Use the array CUSTOMER$ for the customer names and the array PURCHASES for the number of purchases. Then enter the names of customers with new purchases, one at a time, checking through the arrays for the proper element to increment. If the customer is a new one, add that person to the file. Follow the last update with the trailer END. Once all of the updating is finished, you can create a new copy of the file CLIENTS.

Step 3. Code the program

```
REM  PROGRAM TO UPDATE THE CUSTOMER FILE CLIENTS
DIM CUSTOMER$(125), PURCHASES(125)

REM ********** READ IN DATA FILE ***********************
GOSUB READCLIENTS

REM *********** UPDATE INFORMATION ******************
GOSUB UPDATE

REM *********** PRINT DATA TO CLIENT FILE **************
GOSUB WRITECLIENTS
END

REM  ********** SUBROUTINE SECTION *******************
READCLIENTS:
OPEN "CLIENTS" FOR INPUT AS #1
N = 0
WHILE NOT EOF(1)
  N = N + 1
  REM FILLING THE ARRAYS FROM THE FILE
  INPUT #1, CUSTOMER$(N), PURCHASES(N)
WEND
CLOSE 1
RETURN
```

```
UPDATE:
PRINT "ENTER CLIENT NAME. USE THE TRAILER END AFTER"
PRINT "THE LAST CLIENT'S NAME."
INPUT "ENTER CLIENT NAME ";N$
WHILE N$ <> "END"
  REM CHECK CLIENT LIST FOR CUSTOMER N$
  I = 1
  WHILE I <= N AND N$ <> CUSTOMER$(I)
    I = I+1
  WEND
  IF N$ <> CUSTOMER$(I) THEN
     N = N + 1
     CUSTOMER$(N) = N$
     PURCHASES(N)=PURCHASES(N)+1
  ELSE
     PURCHASES(I)=PURCHASES(I)+1
  END IF
  INPUT "ENTER CLIENT NAME ";N$
WEND
RETURN

WRITECLIENTS:
OPEN "CLIENTS" FOR OUTPUT AS #2
FOR I = 1 TO N
 PRINT #2, CUSTOMER$(I); ","; PURCHASES(I)
NEXT I
CLOSE 2
RETURN
```

Further Notes on Program 41:

1. It is assumed that the current number of customers is less than 100. The DIM statement dimensions each array to 125 cells to allow the program to handle new buyers up to a total of 125 customers.
2. Note that the variable N counts the number of customers in the file and PURCHASES(I) is the number of purchases made by customer CUSTOMER$(I).
3. Your original goal was to update the existing data file CLIENTS. However, what you actually accomplished is the creation in the subroutine WRITECLIENTS of an entirely new data file called CLIENTS.

A word of caution is in order here. Suppose while you are updating an existing data file you find out that your program has a logic error and that the new copy of the file is incorrect. After making the correction in your program, you plan to start updating all over again. However, the old file is now replaced by your updated incorrect file! The old copy is gone! To avoid destroying the only correct copy of the file, you could create a new file "NCLIENTS" (for New CLIENTS) in Program 41. Then, if the new file is satisfactory, CLIENTS could be renamed OCLIENTS (for Old CLIENTS) and NCLIENTS then named CLIENTS. (You could use the DOS COPY command here.) In this way you can avoid the inherent danger of destroying good data when updating a data file.

The next program is designed to update a personal expense file.

<u>Program 42.</u>

<u>Step 1.</u> Describe the problem.

You want to keep a running total of your personal income and expenses. This file can be updated monthly, weekly, or in whatever time periods you choose. On the positive side of your "ledger" are the categories

1. PRESENT CASH
2. SALARY
3. MISCELLANEOUS INCOME
4. TOTAL AVAILABLE

Your expenditures include the categories:

5. RENT
6. FOOD
7. UTILITIES
8. CONTRIBUTIONS
9. INSURANCE
10. PERSONAL
11. CAR UPKEEP
12. SAVINGS
13. CLOTHES
14. MEDICAL
15. ENTERTAINMENT
16. MISCELLANEOUS EXPENSES
17. TOTAL EXPENSES

<u>Step 2.</u> Design the logic of the solution.

Use two arrays, CATEGORY$ for the category descriptions and AMOUNT for the (numerical) dollar amounts. The array CATEGORY$ will contain the 17 descriptions listed above. The PRESENT CASH (item 1) category represents the NET CASH from the previous updating of the file. After the array elements are read from the file, update the cash available (items 2–4). This month's cash available (INCOME) is also totaled. To update expenses, enter amounts to add to the values of items 5–17. This month's expenses are totaled in TOTALEXPENSE. The current month's cash BALANCE is found by subtracting TOTALEXPENSE from INCOME. The NET CASH is then found by adding last month's PRESENT CASH (item 1) to this month's BALANCE. Print out the results, skipping one line between the TOTAL AVAILABLE category and the expense categories, and another line between TOTAL EXPENSES and NET CASH.

Step 3. Code the Program.

```
' PROGRAM TO ANSWER THE QUESTION WHERE DOES THE MONEY GO?
' THIS PROGRAM UPDATES A PERSONAL EXPENSE FILE
' VARIABLE DICTIONARY
' ** AMOUNT(1) =  PRESENT CASH
' ** AMOUNT(2) =  SALARY
' ** AMOUNT(3) =  MISCELLANEOUS INCOME
' ** AMOUNT(4) =  TOTAL AVAILABLE CASH
' ** AMOUNT(5) =  RENT
' ** AMOUNT(6) =  FOOD
' ** AMOUNT(7) =  UTILITIES
' ** AMOUNT(8) =  CONTRIBUTIONS
' ** AMOUNT(9) =  INSURANCE
' ** AMOUNT(10) = PERSONAL
' ** AMOUNT(11) = CAR UPKEEP
' ** AMOUNT(12) = SAVINGS
' ** AMOUNT(13) = CLOTHES
' ** AMOUNT(14) = MEDICAL
' ** AMOUNT(15) = ENTERTAINMENT
' ** AMOUNT(16) = MISCELLANEOUS EXPENSES
' ** AMOUNT(17) = TOTAL EXPENSES

DIM CATEGORY$(17), AMOUNT(17)
' *************** READ IN EXPENSE FILE ********************
GOSUB GETINFO
' ************ PRINT OUT CURRENT CATEGORIES ****************
GOSUB PRINTCATEGORIES
' ************** UPDATE INCOME CATEGORIES ******************
GOSUB INCOME
' ***************** UPDATE EXPENDITURES *******************
GOSUB EXPENSES
' ******** PRINT OUT CURRENT UPDATED CATEGORIES ************
GOSUB FINALREPORT
' ***** SAVE CURRENT VALUES IN A NEW FILE, NEXPENSE ********
GOSUB SAVECURRENT
END

GETINFO:
OPEN "EXPENSE" FOR INPUT AS #1
FOR I = 1 TO 17
  INPUT #1, CATEGORY$(I), AMOUNT(I)
NEXT I
CLOSE 1
RETURN

PRINTCATEGORIES:
```

```
PRINT “THE CATEGORIES TO UPDATE ARE:”
A$ = “\_________________________\” + SPACE$(9) + “$####.##”
FOR I = 1 TO 17
  PRINT USING A$; CATEGORY$(I), AMOUNT(I)
NEXT I
PRINT
RETURN

INCOME:
PRINT “UPDATE CASH ON HAND”
PRINT
INCOME = 0
FOR I = 2 TO 3
  PRINT “ENTER NEW ”; CATEGORY$(I)
  INPUT PAY
  INCOME = INCOME + PAY
  AMOUNT(I) = AMOUNT(I) + PAY
  AMOUNT(4) = AMOUNT(4) + PAY
NEXT I
RETURN

EXPENSES:
PRINT “UPDATE EXPENSES”
PRINT
TOTALEXPENSE = 0
FOR I = 5 TO 16
  PRINT “ENTER EXPENSE FOR ”; CATEGORY$(I)
  INPUT EXPENSE
  AMOUNT(I) = AMOUNT(I) + EXPENSE
  AMOUNT(17) = AMOUNT(17) + EXPENSE
  TOTALEXPENSE = TOTALEXPENSE + EXPENSE
NEXT I
PRINT
RETURN

FINALREPORT:
BALANCE = INCOME - TOTALEXPENSE
PRINT USING A$; “THIS MONTH’S BALANCE”, BALANCE
PRINT
PRINT “THE CUMULATIVE TOTALS:”
FOR I = 2 TO 4
  PRINT USING A$; CATEGORY$(I), AMOUNT(I)
NEXT I
PRINT
FOR I = 5 TO 17
  PRINT USING A$; CATEGORY$(I), AMOUNT(I)
NEXT I
```

```
AMOUNT(1) = AMOUNT(1) + BALANCE
PRINT USING A$; "NET CASH"; AMOUNT(1)
RETURN

SAVECURRENT:
OPEN "NEXPENSE" FOR OUTPUT AS #1
FOR I = 1 TO 17
  PRINT #1, CATEGORY$(I); ","; AMOUNT(I)
NEXT I
CLOSE 1
RETURN
```

Output:

```
THE CATEGORIES TO UPDATE ARE:
PRESENT CASH                    $   0.00
SALARY                          $   0.00
MISCELLANEOUS INCOME            $   0.00
TOTAL AVAILABLE                 $   0.00
RENT                            $   0.00
FOOD                            $   0.00
UTILITIES                       $   0.00
CONTRIBUTIONS                   $   0.00
INSURANCE                       $   0.00
PERSONAL                        $   0.00
CAR UPKEEP                      $   0.00
SAVINGS                         $   0.00
CLOTHES                         $   0.00
MEDICAL                         $   0.00
ENTERTAINMENT                   $   0.00
MISCELLANEOUS EXPENSES          $   0.00
TOTAL EXPENSES                  $   0.00

UPDATE CASH ON HAND

ENTER NEW SALARY
? 1800
ENTER NEW MISCELLANEOUS INCOME
? 125

UPDATE EXPENSES

ENTER EXPENSE FOR RENT
? 350
ENTER EXPENSE FOR FOOD
? 246.23
ENTER EXPENSE FOR UTILITIES
```

```
? 188.69
ENTER EXPENSE FOR CONTRIBUTIONS
? 80
ENTER EXPENSE FOR INSURANCE
? 141.1
ENTER EXPENSE FOR PERSONAL
? 45
ENTER EXPENSE FOR CAR UPKEEP
? 78.9
ENTER EXPENSE FOR SAVINGS
? 250
ENTER EXPENSE FOR CLOTHES
? 43.99
ENTER EXPENSE FOR MEDICAL
? 28
ENTER EXPENSE FOR ENTERTAINMENT
? 30
ENTER EXPENSE FOR MISCELLANEOUS EXPENSES
? 41.56

THIS MONTH'S BALANCE                  $ 401.53

THE CUMULATIVE TOTALS:
SALARY                                $1800.00
MISCELLANEOUS INCOME                  $ 125.00
TOTAL AVAILABLE                       $1925.00

RENT                                  $ 350.00
FOOD                                  $ 246.23
UTILITIES                             $ 188.69
CONTRIBUTIONS                         $  80.00
INSURANCE                             $ 141.10
PERSONAL                              $  45.00
CAR UPKEEP                            $  78.90
SAVINGS                               $ 250.00
CLOTHES                               $  43.99
MEDICAL                               $  28.00
ENTERTAINMENT                         $  30.00
MISCELLANEOUS EXPENSES                $  41.56
TOTAL EXPENSES                        $1523.47
NET CASH                              $ 401.53
```

Note that this program follows the word of caution stated at the end of the last program in that data is written to a new file called NEXPENSE (for New EXPENSE). Once you are satisfied that the new file is correct, EXPENSE can be renamed OEXPENSE (for Old EXPENSE) and then NEXPENSE can be renamed EXPENSE using the DOS COPY command. The data file EXPENSE would then be ready for the next update, and that's what you'll do next. A second run of this program follows.

Output:

```
THE CATEGORIES TO UPDATE ARE:
PRESENT CASH                          $ 401.53
SALARY                                $1800.00
MISCELLANEOUS INCOME                  $ 125.00
TOTAL AVAILABLE                       $1925.00
RENT                                  $ 350.00
FOOD                                  $ 246.23
UTILITIES                             $ 188.69
CONTRIBUTIONS                         $   80.00
INSURANCE                             $ 141.10
PERSONAL                              $   45.00
CAR UPKEEP                            $   78.90
SAVINGS                               $ 250.00
CLOTHES                               $   43.99
MEDICAL                               $   28.00
ENTERTAINMENT                         $   30.00
MISCELLANEOUS EXPENSES                $   41.56
TOTAL EXPENSES                        $1523.47

UPDATE CASH ON HAND

ENTER NEW SALARY
? 1800
ENTER NEW MISCELLANEOUS INCOME
? 0

UPDATE EXPENSES

ENTER EXPENSE FOR RENT
? 350
ENTER EXPENSE FOR FOOD
? 261.4
ENTER EXPENSE FOR UTILITIES
? 213.9
ENTER EXPENSE FOR CONTRIBUTIONS
? 100
ENTER EXPENSE FOR INSURANCE
? 168
ENTER EXPENSE FOR PERSONAL
? 64.75
ENTER EXPENSE FOR CAR UPKEEP
? 198.7
ENTER EXPENSE FOR SAVINGS
? 250
ENTER EXPENSE FOR CLOTHES
```

```
? 185
ENTER EXPENSE FOR MEDICAL
? 66
ENTER EXPENSE FOR ENTERTAINMENT
? 40
ENTER EXPENSE FOR MISCELLANEOUS EXPENSES
? 32

THIS MONTH'S BALANCE                    $-129.75

THE CUMULATIVE TOTALS:
SALARY                                  $3600.00
MISCELLANEOUS INCOME                    $ 125.00
TOTAL AVAILABLE                         $3725.00

RENT                                    $ 700.00
FOOD                                    $ 507.63
UTILITIES                               $ 402.59
CONTRIBUTIONS                           $ 180.00
INSURANCE                               $ 309.10
PERSONAL                                $ 109.75
CAR UPKEEP                              $ 277.60
SAVINGS                                 $ 500.00
CLOTHES                                 $ 228.99
MEDICAL                                 $  94.00
ENTERTAINMENT                           $  70.00
MISCELLANEOUS EXPENSES                  $  73.56
TOTAL EXPENSES                          $3453.22

NET CASH                                $ 271.78
```

Further Notes on Program 42:

1. A variable dictionary, such as the one listed at the beginning of this program, becomes very useful in lengthy programs.
2. For more flexibility, you can use a character variable for the filename in the OPEN statement. Therefore, instead of

   ```
   OPEN "EXPENSE" FOR INPUT AS #1
   ```

   you could use

   ```
   INPUT "ENTER THE NAME OF THE FILE TO BE UPDATED ";FILENAME$
   OPEN FILENAME$ AS INPUT #1
   ```

   Likewise, when saving the updated categories, you could use

   ```
   INPUT "ENTER FILENAME TO SAVE CATEGORIES ";FILENAME$
   OPEN FILENAME$ AS OUTPUT #1
   ```

3. The two successive runs update the data file twice. Note the non-zero values in the file at the beginning of the second run.
4. The format established with A$ provides 22 spaces for an alphanumeric string and a sequence of nine spaces followed by a numerical format allowing for a fixed dollar sign and zero fill with a maximum value of 9999.99.
5. You are invited to change, add, or delete categories to customize the file for personal use.
6. Those who have worked with spreadsheet application packages will realize that this program simulates the manipulation of values in a spreadsheet.
7. You can change this program so that a month-by-month total of assets and expenditures is provided. The array AMOUNT in our program would be replaced with a two-dimensional array with 18 rows and 13 columns (one for totals). This modification of Program 42 is left as an exercise.

D. REVIEW EXERCISES

1. List the four fundamental ways that variables can be assigned values in a QuickBASIC program.
2. Using a data file named SCORES, write a QuickBASIC statement to
   (a) open this file for output,
   (b) close the output file,
   (c) open this file for input.
3. What is the difference in the following statements?

```
PRINT N
PRINT #1, N
```

4. The following program is supposed to create a file of names and numbers and then print out that data. However, there are problems with this code. Find and correct the errors in the code.

```
OPEN "LIST" FOR INPUT AS #1
FOR I = 1 TO 3
  PRINT "ENTER LAST NAME AND NUMERICAL VALUE"
  INPUT N$, VALUE
  PRINT #1, N$, ",", VALUE
NEXT I
FOR I = 1 TO 3
  INPUT #1, N$
  INPUT #1, VALUE
  PRINT N$, VALUE
NEXT I
CLOSE #1
END
```

E. LAB EXERCISES

1. In the Lab Exercise of Chapter Five, you worked on a mailing list of customers of an appliance store. Let's modify that exercise so that a customer's name, local address, city, state, zip code, date of last purchase, and category of last purchase are stored in a record in a data file that you will create called CUSTOMERS.

   Costello Annette,3419 Monroe St.,Bellwood,IL,60104,10/18/90,19
   Adams Mark,601 Waldron St.,Lafayette,IN,47906,1/7/91,23
   Wilson Deborah,2900 Sienna,Muncie,IN,47304,7/1/90,1
   Fox Tim,5929 Park St.,Burlington,WI,51624,5/2/91,17
   Connors Mike,1200 Hoyt,Chicago,IL,60613,11/10/90,35

   Note that commas separate data items, no comma is used in the name field, and no extra spaces are needed between fields. Write the QuickBASIC statement to open the file CUSTOMERS to accept data from your program.

   ____

   Using the variables PERSON$, STREET$, CITY$, STATE$, ZIP$, DAY$, and CATEGORY, enter the above five records into your program and then write them to your file. Be sure to insert commas into your file and print each record on a single line in the file. Show your code below.

   ____
   ____
   ____
   ____
   ____
   ____
   ____
   ____

   Be sure to close your file and save this program under the name CREATE. If you check your directory, you should find this file (listed as CREATE.BAS) as well as CUSTOMERS.

2. Suppose that you want to know which customers have purchased a product in category 19, 23, or 40. You can read information from the data file CUSTOMERS into a program and then print a listing of the name and address for those satisfying these conditions. To begin, open the file for input into the program. Write the appropriate statement.

   ____

   Next write the code including a single INPUT statement that enters the complete records into your program. Use the same variable names as in Lab Exercise 1. (No need for arrays here.)

   ____
   ____
   ____

Finally, insert into your program the necessary statements to print out the name and address of those customers who have purchased items in category 19, 23, or 40. The name, street, city, state, and zip code should be printed starting in positions 1, 21, 35, 45, and 48, respectively. Show the complete program below.

3. Modify the program you have written for this lab to print out those customers whose last purchase was made after 12/31/90. Write the new statement(s) below.

4. Modify the program you currently have for this lab to print out those customers whose zip code begins with a 4 or a 6 (to identify customers from certain sections of the country). Write the new statement(s) below.

F. PROGRAMMING PROBLEMS

1. In Program 41, the number of transactions in the file CLIENTS is always incremented by one when a customer makes a purchase. Enhance this program by incorporating the following:
   (a) allow the number of purchases to be increased by more than one to handle the situation in which a customer has made several purchases since the last time the file was updated,
   (b) allow the number of purchases to be decreased if the customer returns an item.

2. Write a program to create a data file called CLASS, where each record contains three fields: student name, first test score, second test score. Use the following data:

TOM SMITH	93	78
AL SULLIVAN	81	92
MARY ALLEN	88	62
JANET CARSON	100	85

3. Using the file CLASS that you created in the last problem, write a program to do the following:
   (a) Print out all student names and scores, with appropriate headings.
   (b) Find the class average on each test and print out these results with appropriate messages.
   (c) After an appropriate heading print out the names of those students who averaged over 90 for both tests.

4. Modify Program 42 so that the user can keep a record of assets and expenditures, with a month-by-month display of data, for a twelve-month period.

5. In Chapter Four, Programming Problem 7, the Whirly Disk inventory distribution was introduced. The part number, cost per item, and the number of units in inventory at each of four warehouses is reproduced here.

Part #	Cost	Warehouse			
		1	2	3	4
1	.67	600	332	241	1000
2	.99	800	92	505	400
3	1.10	225	432	392	125
4	4.00	88	99	362	428
5	.25	85	89	125	320

   (a) Create a file INVENTORY to store the above data. Incorporate into your program a segment that reads and displays the contents of the file.
   (b) Print a report showing the part number, the cost, and the total number of units in inventory across the country.
   (c) Print a report listing each part and the total dollars tied up in inventory across the country.
   (d) Update the file to incorporate the following changes in inventory:
      (i) 200 #1 parts are used from warehouse 1.
      (ii) 300 #2 parts are transferred from warehouse 1 to warehouse 2.
      (iii) 400 #5 parts are added to the inventory in warehouses 1 and 2.

Print out the latest version of INVENTORY.

INDEX